Grammar

Michael Swan is a writer specializing in
English language teaching and reference
materials. He is a Visiting Professor at
St Mary's University College,
Twickenham.

For Catherine

Published in this series:

Guy Cook: *Applied Linguistics*
Rod Ellis: *Second Language Acquisition*
Claire Kramsch: *Language and Culture*
Tim McNamara: *Language Testing*
Peter Roach: *Phonetics*
Herbert Schendl: *Historical Linguistics*
Thomas Scovel: *Psycholinguistics*
Bernard Spolsky: *Sociolinguistics*
Peter Verdonk: *Stylistics*
H.G.Widdowson: *Linguistics*
George Yule: *Pragmatics*

Oxford Introductions to Language Study

Series Editor H.G. Widdowson

Grammar

Michael Swan

OXFORD

UNIVERSITY PRESS

OXFORD

UNIVERSITY PRESS

Great Clarendon Street, Oxford OX2 6DP

Oxford University Press is a department of the University of Oxford.
It furthers the University's objective of excellence in research, scholarship,
and education by publishing worldwide in

Oxford New York

Auckland Cape Town Dar es Salaam Hong Kong Karachi
Kuala Lumpur Madrid Melbourne Mexico City Nairobi
New Delhi Shanghai Taipei Toronto

With offices in

Argentina Austria Brazil Chile Czech Republic France Greece
Guatemala Hungary Italy Japan Poland Portugal Singapore
South Korea Switzerland Thailand Turkey Ukraine Vietnam

OXFORD and OXFORD ENGLISH are registered trade marks of
Oxford University Press in the UK and in certain other countries

© Oxford University Press 2005

The moral rights of the author have been asserted

Database right Oxford University Press (maker)

First published 2005
2015
10 9 8 7

ISBN: 978 0 19 437241 1

Printed in China

Contents

Preface

Purpose

What justification might there be for a series of introductions to language study? After all, linguistics is already well served with introductory texts: expositions and explanations which are comprehensive, authoritative, and excellent in their way. Generally speaking, however, their way is the essentially academic one of providing a detailed initiation into the discipline of linguistics, and they tend to be lengthy and technical: appropriately so, given their purpose. But they can be quite daunting to the novice. There is also a need for a more general and gradual introduction to language: transitional texts which will ease people into an understanding of complex ideas. This series of introductions is designed to serve this need.

Their purpose, therefore, is not to supplant but to support the more academically oriented introductions to linguistics: to prepare the conceptual ground. They are based on the belief that it is an advantage to have a broad map of the terrain sketched out before one considers its more specific features on a smaller scale, a general context in reference to which the detail makes sense. It is sometimes the case that students are introduced to detail without it being made clear what it is a detail of. Clearly, a general understanding of ideas is not sufficient: there needs to be closer scrutiny. But equally, close scrutiny can be myopic and meaningless unless it is related to the larger view. Indeed it can be said that the precondition of more particular enquiry is an awareness of what, in general, the particulars are about. This series is designed to provide this large-scale view of different areas of language study. As such it can serve as preliminary to (and precondition for) the more specific and specialized enquiry which students of linguistics are required to undertake.

But the series is not only intended to be helpful to such students. There are many people who take an interest in language without being academically engaged in linguistics *per se*. Such people may recognize the importance of understanding language for their own lines of enquiry, or for their own practical purposes, or quite simply for making them aware of something which figures so centrally in their everyday lives. If linguistics has revealing and relevant things to say about language, this should presumably not be a privileged revelation, but one accessible to people other than linguists. These books have been so designed as to accommodate these broader interests too: they are meant to be introductions to language more generally as well as to linguistics as a discipline.

Design

The books in the series are all cut to the same basic pattern. There are four parts: Survey, Readings, References, and Glossary.

Survey

This is a summary overview of the main features of the area of language study concerned: its scope and principles of enquiry, its basic concerns and key concepts. These are expressed and explained in ways which are intended to make them as accessible as possible to people who have no prior knowledge or expertise in the subject. The Survey is written to be readable and is uncluttered by the customary scholarly references. In this sense, it is simple. But it is not simplistic. Lack of specialist expertise does not imply an inability to understand or evaluate ideas. Ignorance means lack of knowledge, not lack of intelligence. The Survey, therefore, is meant to be challenging. It draws a map of the subject area in such a way as to stimulate thought and to invite a critical participation in the exploration of ideas. This kind of conceptual cartography has its dangers of course: the selection of what is significant, and the manner of its representation, will not be to the liking of everybody, particularly not, perhaps, to some of those inside the discipline. But these surveys are written in the belief/ that there must be an alternative to a technical account on the one hand and an idiot's guide on the other if linguistics is to be made relevant to people in the wider world.

Readings

Some people will be content to read, and perhaps re-read, the summary Survey. Others will want to pursue the subject and so will use the Survey as the preliminary for more detailed study. The Readings provide the necessary transition. For here the reader is presented with texts extracted from the specialist literature. The purpose of these Readings is quite different from the Survey. It is to get readers to focus on the specifics of what is said, and how it is said, in these source texts. Questions are provided to further this purpose: they are designed to direct attention to points in each text, how they compare across texts, and how they deal with the issues discussed in the Survey. The idea is to give readers an initial familiarity with the more specialist idiom of the linguistics literature, where the issues might not be so readily accessible, and to encourage them into close critical reading.

References

One way of moving into more detailed study is through the Readings. Another is through the annotated References in the third section of each book. Here there is a selection of works (books and articles) for further reading. Accompanying comments indicate how these deal in more detail with the issues discussed in the different chapters of the Survey.

Glossary

Certain terms in the Survey appear in bold. These are terms used in a special or technical sense in the discipline. Their meanings are made clear in the discussion, but they are also explained in the Glossary at the end of each book. The Glossary is cross-referenced to the Survey, and therefore serves at the same time as an index. This enables readers to locate the term and what it signifies in the more general discussion, thereby, in effect, using the Survey as a summary work of reference.

Use

The series has been designed so as to be flexible in use. Each title is separate and self-contained, with only the basic format in common. The four sections of the format, as described here, can be drawn upon and combined in different ways, as required by the needs, or interests, of different readers. Some may be content with the Survey and the Glossary and may not want to follow up the suggested References. Some may not wish to venture into the Readings. Again, the Survey might be considered as appropriate preliminary reading for a course in applied linguistics or teacher education, and the Readings more appropriate for seminar discussion during the course. In short, the notion an introduction will mean different things to different people, but in all cases the concern is to provide access to specialist knowledge and stimulate an awareness of its significance. This series as a whole has been designed to provide this access and promote this awareness in respect to different areas of language study.

H. G. WIDDOWSON

Author's Introduction

If grammar is dull, as it often is, the problem may be one of focus. Students commonly learn about such phenomena as pronouns or relative clauses, or study the strange ways in which foreign languages organize their grammatical affairs, without gaining very much sense of why languages should have these features. It is rather as if one studied, say, a dragonfly purely by looking at small parts of the insect through a microscope. A better approach, surely, would be to start with a view of the dragonfly as a whole, and to see how the parts contribute to the systems that enable the creature to develop, maintain its physical integrity, move about, and reproduce. In this perspective a certain amount of detail, introduced judiciously, might well prove to be illustrative and illuminating rather than tedious and baffling. So it is with language.

This is not a book about English grammar, or that of any other language. Nor does it offer a linguistic theory to compete with the many already in existence. Its purpose is to provide a wide-angle, low-magnification look at grammar in general. It asks, and attempts to answer, some rather simple-looking questions. What, in fact, is grammar? Why does it get so complicated? What are the different ways in which the world's languages exploit it? How does it relate to other aspects of language, and to the outside world? How is it involved in language change? What are the implications of 'grammatical correctness' for education and society? What, if anything, do we know about how grammar is represented in the mind and stored in the brain?

Language is what distinguishes us as human beings. It is our greatest cognitive achievement, and the foundation of all our other achievements. Its separate realizations—individual languages—are beautiful structures. At the centre of their workings is the cluster of systems we call grammar: simple in principle, complex and endlessly fascinating in practice. I hope that this book will help to convey some of that fascination.

Author's Acknowledgements

It has been well said that to steal from one person is plagiarism, but that to steal from everybody is research. This book is based on extensive research. Someone who sets out to write about the way grammar works in the world's 6,000 or so languages, and who speaks three of them, needs all the help he can get. I have therefore drawn heavily and unashamedly on academic treatments of the topics I deal with, and of the languages I refer to for illustration. To the authors and editors of these publications, whose work has made mine possible, I extend my respectful thanks. The most important of these debts are reflected in Section 2, Readings, on pages 81–108.

I am also most grateful to a number of individuals who have been kind enough to supply me with information, resources, insights, suggestions, and opinions: Natasha Bochorishvili, Jie Dong, Adrian du Plessis, Pauline Foster, Mohammed Hamza, Hideo Hibino, Juan Hu, Dick Hudson, Ken Hyland, Kenji Kashino, Tomoko Morikawa, Des O'Sullivan, Julia Sallabank, Bernard Smith, Penny Ur, Bruce Wade, Xiaoyan Wan (Erica), Ying-Chieh Cathy Wu, and Annemarie Young.

Finally, I am deeply indebted to Catherine Walter and Henry Widdowson, both of whom have read the entire typescript and contributed wise and constructive advice. This has greatly improved the book; all remaining defects are entirely my responsibility.

MICHAEL SWAN

Survey

1

What is grammar?

What is grammar for?

The word 'grammar' can mean very different things to different people—many of them negative. For example:

- something that young people today are not taught properly at school, as a result of which the language is going to the dogs
- a collection of arcane terminology: 'auxiliary', 'past participle', 'relative clause', 'complement'
- a cluster of prohibitions that make people worry about whether they speak their own language properly ('Don't say *between you and I*'; 'Don't split infinitives'; '*Less people* is wrong; you should say *fewer people*'; and so on)
- a galaxy of apparently arbitrary **rules** which make foreign languages unnecessarily difficult and seem to get in the way of natural communication: for example, French **genders**; German word order; Russian **case** endings; **honorific** verb forms in Japanese
- a large dusty book full of any of the above.

Not everybody, of course, has such a simple view of the matter. But even if you feel you know pretty well what grammar is, you might not find it easy to define. 'What is grammar?' is the kind of question that seems easy to answer until somebody asks it. Reference books are not a great deal of help—most dictionary definitions simply say something like 'the rules for combining words into sentences'. Not only is this seriously incomplete as a definition (grammar does many other things besides sentence-building); it also gives no indication of the function of grammar—as if one defined a bus as a 'large vehicle constructed on one or two levels', without mentioning that it is used for public transport.

To understand what grammar is, we really need to know what it is for. Why do we need 'rules for combining words into sentences' anyway? Couldn't we manage well enough just by saying the words? This is a perfectly sensible question, and an excellent starting point for our enquiry. The best way to understand what grammar is, what it does, and why it is necessary, is in fact to try to imagine language without it.

Language without grammar

Nobody knows how language originated, but let us carry out a thought experiment. Suppose that you are an intelligent primate that would like to invent a rich communication system. There are various possible ways to signal information, some of which you already use to a limited extent: cries and grunts, facial expressions, gestures. For your new system, you decide that cries and grunts are the most effective option: you can get more variety into vocal signs, and they are not dependent on visibility (so they will work round corners and in the dark).

At first sight, it might look as if the obvious thing to do would be for you and your companions to devise a distinctive vocal sign—let's call it a 'word'—for each of the things in your world. (For this to work, you would also need to create a phonological system, but that is not relevant to the present discussion.) So you invent words for your mother, the other mothers in the tribe, the cave mouth, the chief of the tribe, the big tree by the river, the river, the rain that is falling just now, your best stone axe, your second-best stone axe, and so on. However, it quickly becomes clear that this will not work. First of all, there are too many things around for a communication system constructed on this basis to be learnable. And secondly, the system only enables you to talk about particular things that you have already paid attention to. You cannot talk, for example, about another tree, a new river that you have discovered, a stranger, or the axe you intend to make.

A more promising approach is to use words to designate classes of things instead of individuals, so that your words for 'tree', 'rain', 'mother', 'axe', 'baby', 'bear', and so on can refer to any tree, any instance of rain, etc. (This is anyway an extension of your existing signalling system, which already consists of a few calls indicating recurrent elements in your world like 'danger', 'panther', 'food', 'enemy'.)

And with an important mental leap, you realize that words can refer not only to people and things, but also to their shared characteristics, like 'big', 'good to eat', 'red', or 'cold'; and to the events, situations, and changes that regularly occur in your world, like 'eat', 'fall', 'run', 'die', 'coming', 'gone'. (Strictly speaking, it probably does not make sense to separate your consciousness of categories from your labelling of them, as if one came before the other; but it simplifies the discussion to look at things in this way.)

Now you are ready to use your new tool. There are three things you and your companions can do with it. First of all, you can draw each other's attention to the existence of something in your environment, or to the fact that you want something, by simply using the appropriate class word ('Bear!', 'Axe!', 'Eat!'). Secondly, when necessary, you can combine words to pin down individual members of classes and make it clear which one you are talking about: if you want to ask for a particular axe, you can produce the equivalent of, for instance, 'axe big'. This is an enormously powerful device—think how the four English words 'your', 'big', 'blue', and 'mug', each of which refers to a class with vast numbers of members, can be put together to immediately identify one particular item. And thirdly, you can combine words to indicate events or states of affairs: 'Fall baby'; 'Rain cold'; 'Bear die'; 'Axe big break'; 'Eat baby acorn'.

You have invented language! Up to a point.

Problems

Your language is, however, rather different from the human languages we are familiar with. For one thing, the order of words has no significance: 'Fall baby' and 'Baby fall' are alternative forms of the same message. And for another, there is only one kind of word ('bear', 'die', and 'cold' are not respectively a noun, a verb, and an adjective—they are just words).

Does this matter? Well, you can certainly do a lot with the language you have, and it is a remarkable advance on your earlier, very limited communication system. However, it has some limitations. There are three in particular:

1 It can be difficult to specify exact meanings in situations involving more than one element. Putting together your words for 'big', 'bear', and 'cave', for example, will not make it clear whether there is a big bear in the cave or a bear in the big cave. Context will often remove the ambiguity, but this will not always be the case.

2 Your language will enable you to identify and talk about things in the world as separate elements, but not to clarify the causal, spatial, and other relationships between them, and these may need to be spelt out. For instance, in a situation where A is doing something to B, you cannot easily make it clear, just by saying the words, who or what is the 'doer' (or 'agent'), and who or what is the 'doee' (or '**patient**'). Again, context or common sense will often make this clear ('Eat baby acorn' can only be sensibly understood in one way), but confusion can easily arise, as in 'Kill brother bear' (remember that as things stand the order of words communicates nothing).

3 And finally, with this system you cannot get beyond requests and affirmative statements—'Bear cave' can convey the fact that there is a bear in the cave, but you have no way of asking whether there is a bear in the cave, or suggesting that there may be, or saying that there is not a bear in the cave.

So you need:
(i) a way of saying what word goes with what—of indicating how general concepts need to be grouped in order to represent particular elements in the world
(ii) a way of expressing agency and other relationships
(iii) a way of indicating the communicative status of your utterances—statement, question, suggestion, negation, or whatever.

You have discovered the need for grammar.

Solving the problems

There are quite a number of ways in which you might meet this need. One approach would be to signal the necessary extra meanings by the way you arrange words. To show what goes with what, for example, you could have a rule that you always put words for connected ideas together, perhaps with pauses between phrases: 'bear big—small cave'. You could refine this—and avoid the need for pauses—by always putting the word for a quality immediately before or immediately after the word for the thing that has the quality: 'bear big'; 'cave small'. Another way of using word order would be to consistently put the expression for an agent or 'doer' earlier or later than other expressions, so that 'brother kill bear' and 'bear kill brother' would have distinct meanings. And again, you could use a different order of phrases for statements and questions: 'Brother kill big bear' versus 'Kill brother big bear?'.

A second strategy would be to alter words in some way to signal their functions. Latin did this: *ursus* and *frater* meant 'bear' and 'brother' as agents; as patients they became *ursum* and *fratrem*. Russian does much the same. This trick—**inflection**—could also be exploited to show what goes with what: related words could all be changed or extended identically. In Latin you could talk about a big bear without needing to put the two words next to each other: if 'bear' was *ursus*, 'big' was *magnus*; if it was *ursum*, 'big' was *magnum*, so the relationship was clear. Pronunciation, too, could indicate the functions of words. To show that a word referred to an agent, for example, you could pronounce the first sound differently; or you could say the word more slowly, or on a higher pitch: *Kill* ^{bear} *brother*. You could also use **intonation** to mark the status of a whole utterance, as we often do in English to indicate that we are asking questions.

Yet another possibility would be to invent new non-referential words that do not label anything in the world, but that are used to show the function of other words. English 'may' is a word of this kind: it indicates that your sentence refers not to a definite fact, but to a possibility. Japanese puts small words—**particles**—after nouns to mean such things as 'topic', 'agent', 'patient', and 'possessor'.

These strategies are all variants on three basic options: ordering, inflection, and the use of **function words**. Once you have selected from these three options the devices you want to use for your language, you have devised a grammar. You now have a human language.

So, to answer the question we started with: grammar is essentially a limited set of devices for expressing certain kinds of necessary meaning that cannot be conveyed by referential vocabulary alone.

2
From simplicity to complexity: word classes and structures

As we have seen, grammar consists in principle of a few devices—ordering, inflection, and the use of function words—which are needed to solve an equally small number of problems: identifying **participant roles**, showing how items belong together, and marking the functions of utterances. How is it, then, that grammar seems so complicated in practice? There are several reasons. One of them is the fact that these basic grammatical devices necessarily bring other features with them. Words naturally divide up into classes related to their functions; they also combine into structures, which themselves combine into higher-level structures.

Word classes

We perceive the world in terms of events and situations, in which people and things participate. Our languages reflect this perspective: they have event/situation words, such as English 'run', 'hit', 'fall', 'be', 'contain', and participant words, such as 'tree', 'water', 'boulder', 'woman', 'car'. We also see people, things, events, and situations as having shared qualities—'old', 'green', 'tired', 'fast', 'good'—so languages have ways of referring to these. And we perceive relationships between the elements in our world: something can be 'inside' or 'above' something else, or happen 'after' or 'before' it, or 'cause' it or 'be caused' by it, and so on. These relationships, too, are reflected in language.

Our categorization of reality does not in itself imply the existence of distinct grammatical word classes or **parts of speech**. 'Hit' and 'boulder' are not grammatically different, a verb and a noun, by virtue of referring to an action and a thing respectively:

they are simply words with different kinds of meaning. What makes 'hit' and 'boulder' belong to different word classes is the need that can arise for grammatical labelling, in order to signal their different functions in communication. For instance, we may have to distinguish the participants in an event. Which is the agent, which is the patient? Did the car hit the boulder or the boulder hit the car? Once a mechanism exists for making this distinction—word order, inflection, or whatever—words naturally fall into at least two functional classes: those that can be labelled as participants (for example, 'boulder', 'food', 'car') and those that cannot (for example, the words for the events/situations themselves: 'hit', 'fall', 'see'). At this point, we are in the domain of grammar. Words like 'boulder', 'food', and 'car' are nouns, with one kind of grammatical behaviour; words like 'hit', 'fall', and 'see' behave in a different way, and are verbs.

All languages distinguish nouns, verbs, and some other classes in this way. Word classes include both **content words**, which refer to elements in the world, and function words, which mainly signal language-internal relationships. There is, however, considerable variation between languages (as we shall see in Chapter 3) in the number and nature of identifiable word classes. Even inside one language, divisions are not always very clear-cut. A classroom account of English parts of speech lists articles, nouns, verbs, adjectives, adverbs, pronouns, prepositions, conjunctions, and interjections. But some of these headings clearly cover more than one kind of word. Words like 'my' and 'this', for example, traditionally classified as adjectives, have little in common with words like 'green', 'difficult', or 'important', and modern grammars assign them to a separate class of determiners. The so-called 'pronoun' category contains a variety of words which behave in rather different ways. Some other words seem to hop about from one class to another: is 'tomorrow' a noun ('Tomorrow is Tuesday') or an adverb ('I'll see you tomorrow')? 'Adverb', in any case, is a miscellaneous class, containing a motley collection of **modifiers** and other items which have little in common except that they do not easily fit into other categories. The number of word classes we define in English will ultimately depend on our purposes—on how fussy we need to be in making our distinctions.

Traditional definitions in terms of meaning ('a noun is the name of a person, place, or thing') are not very helpful, though they contain a sort of one-way truth: things are usually encoded as nouns, even if nouns do not necessarily refer to things. It is grammatical function, and not meaning alone, that determines word class; indeed, a particular meaning can often be expressed through different word classes according to how we need to construct an utterance. If we want to report volcanic activity, we are likely to use a verb: 'Mount Karhel *erupted* last night'. But in referring to this event as a participant in a further process, we cannot simply say, in English at least, *'Karhel erupted was heard 800 miles away'. Changing the word class solves the problem: 'The *eruption* was heard 800 miles away'.

Unclear word-class boundaries also reflect the unavoidable mismatch between language and the world. It would be convenient if our linguistic code coincided neatly with our perceptions, so that elements in our experience could be unproblematically assigned to linguistic categories, with 'things' consistently coded as nouns, 'events' and 'situations' as verbs, 'qualities' as adjectives, and so on. Unsurprisingly, this is not what happens. The world is enormous and massively complex, and the categories through which we perceive it flow into each other; a tree is certainly a 'thing', but what about rain or fire: are these things or processes? Is 'up' a quality, a relation, or a state? It is simply impossible to map everything we experience tidily onto a small number of word classes: there are far more kinds of element in the world than we have linguistic or conceptual boxes to put them in. Inevitably, therefore, the dividing lines between word-class categories are fuzzy and are drawn in different places in different languages.

Code and message: from words to phrases

In a rough-and-ready analogy, we might describe language as a *code* which is used to construct *messages*. The words belonging to a language are code items; aside from names like 'Annie' or 'Somalia', they refer mostly to general concepts: 'table', 'selection', 'fall', 'think', 'yellow', 'old', 'my', 'in', 'because'. Language in use, on the other hand, typically refers to particulars. Our messages are about specific tables, or groups of tables, or types of table; about this or that instance of falling, thinking, yellowness, or 'in-ness'. How does the transition work? How do we make the switch from general to particular?

Context may bridge the gap. If I say 'Salt, please' across the table, the code item 'salt' functions effectively as a message. On the other hand, if you are upstairs, and I want you to bring me down a particular sweater, saying 'Sweater, please' will not get me what I want. I have several sweaters, and the code item will not serve as a message item. What I do is to combine several items from the code, and ask you, say, to bring 'my old yellow sweater'. Each of the four categories 'my', 'old', 'yellow', and 'sweater' has a great many members, but they intersect in only one instance: the particular sweater that I want.

Combinations like 'my old yellow sweater'—**phrases**—are the units of language as message, just as words are the units of language as code. An utterance is not simply a string of words, therefore: it is a sequence of phrases, each of which identifies an element in the situation that the utterance is designed to communicate about. The grammar of sentences operates accordingly. If we ask who did something, the answer will typically be a **noun phrase**, not a noun: 'that old man', not 'man'. If we ask where something is happening, we can expect a prepositional phrase: not 'in', but 'in the town hall'. Pronouns refer to phrases, not words: in 'The doctor said she was baffled', 'she' means 'the doctor', not just 'the' or 'doctor'. Changes in word order generally involve moving whole phrases: we can change the balance of 'Mrs Porter came round the corner' by saying 'Round the corner came Mrs Porter', but not *'Porter round the corner came Mrs'. Even where grammatical processes split phrases (as when English moves the first part of a compound verb to make a question: 'you have seen' → 'have you seen?'), these processes are sensitive to the position and internal structure of phrases. (It is of course possible for a phrase to consist of a single word, like the three in 'cats like fish', but these are still phrases—it just happens that the noun phrases in this case have empty determiner and modifier slots, while the **verb phrase** has no **auxiliary**.)

Phrases typically appear as 'clumps', with their constituent words juxtaposed, and they may be further tied together by intonation contours, or separated off by pauses. However, this is not always the case, especially where constituents are linked by their form. Classical Latin writers often separated adjectives from their nouns, for example, for stylistic effect, as in this line from Horace:

*Vitae summa brevis **spem** nos vetat   incohare   **longam.***
Of life span   short **hope** us   forbids to undertake **long.**
(The shortness of life stops us forming **long-term hopes.**)

(*Spem* and *longam*, though separated by three words, are both accusative feminine singular in form, and therefore—to a Roman reader—immediately identifiable as constituting a phrase.) German notoriously breaks up verb phrases, removing infinitives or past participles to the ends of **clauses**. As Mark Twain put it: 'They take part of a verb and put it down here, like a stake, and they take the other part of it and put it away over yonder like another stake, and between these two limits they just shovel in German'.

Ich habe meine Mutter seit   Weihnachten mindestens
I   have my   mother since Christmas   at least

dreimal   besucht.
three times visited.

Clauses

A single phrase can constitute a message: for example, 'More coffee?' or 'The police!'. Usually, however, we need to give more precise information about the situations or processes that we are communicating about. This involves combining phrases into higher-level structures: clauses. A typical clause will contain at the very minimum a verb phrase (VP) of one or more words, and one or more noun phrases (NPs) identifying the participants in the relevant event or situation. (I am using the term 'verb phrase' to refer to a word group consisting of a main verb together with any auxiliaries. Some grammarians use the term differently, to include the verb group together with any objects or complements.) Circumstantial information (for example, details of time or place) will require other elements, such as (in English) adverb phrases (APs) or prepositional phrases (PPs).

```
NP          VP          NP
```
[Your dog] [has dug up] [all my daffodils].

```
PP                      NP          VP      AP
```
[In the afternoon] [the group] [walked] [quite slowly]

```
PP
```
[up to the hut].

Subjects and objects

Clause structure may indicate **participant roles**, such as agent and patient. English typically distinguishes these through the grammatical categories of **subject** and **object**, which have different positions in the clause.

```
NP(S)    VP  NP(O)          NP(S)           VP  NP(O)
```
[The car] [hit] [the boulder].   [The boulder] [hit] [the car].

Where there are more than two participants, English establishes different categories of object—direct and indirect—with the more indirect relationship marked either by a preposition ('I gave £500 *to the hospital*') or by position ('I gave *the hospital* £500'). Subjects and objects are also sometimes distinguished by their form ('I'/'me', 'they'/'them'), and subjects, unlike objects, may require verb **agreement** (we say '*the cat catches* mice' but '*cats catch* mice').

The concepts of 'subject' and 'object' are somewhat elusive (and there may be languages in which these are not grammatical categories). Although agents are generally grammaticalized as subjects, most English subjects are not actually agents. Take, for instance, the sentences 'I don't enjoy opera'; 'My father has a bad cold'; 'Several people saw the accident'. In none of these is there an agent–patient relationship, where one participant does something to another. English (like many languages) takes the grammatical structure 'subject–verb–object' established for agent–patient scenarios, and imposes it on other configurations, such as 'experiencer–thing experienced' or 'perceiver–thing perceived', conventionally encoding one participant-type as subject and the other as object. Whatever the exact configuration, animate participants are statistically most likely to be selected as subjects, and people most of all, in conformity with our cognitive preference for human-centred representations of the world. Verbs generally reflect this bias in their **selection criteria**: 'enjoy' and 'see' both require an animate participant as subject. The bias can be overridden for particular **discourse** purposes (see Chapter 5), for instance, by choosing a verb with different selection criteria ('Opera doesn't appeal to me') or by passivizing ('The accident was seen by several people').

Strictly speaking, participant roles do not always need to be specified grammatically. This information often emerges naturally from the context and our knowledge of the world. If somebody said 'Threw the TV John's father through the window' or 'The accident saw several people', we would be in no real doubt regarding the structure of the event, though we might need time to cope with the unfamiliar word order. TV sets don't throw people; accidents can't see. However, we process language more easily if its organization follows fixed and predictable patterns, and the **redundancy** generated by over-explicitness adds to comprehensibility. Consequently, English makes its speakers structure almost all their sentences, regardless of need, as if these were potentially ambiguous agent–patient utterances requiring grammatically-marked subjects. This extends even to processes with only one participant. In the nursery rhyme 'London Bridge is falling down', the phrase 'London Bridge' is marked as subject by both position and verb agreement, even though there is no need to specify the bridge's role (since there are no competing noun phrases) and it is, of course, no kind of 'agent'. (In some languages, such as Basque, 'London Bridge' would, in fact, have the same morphological case-marking, in the equivalent sentence, as the object of a **transitive** verb.) When a process has nothing that we can sensibly call a participant, and therefore no candidate for the subject slot, English invents one: we say 'It's raining', 'It's late'. Not all languages force everything so rigidly into the subject–verb–(object) mould: in both Dakota (a Native American language) and Lisu (a Burmese language), for example, subjects and objects are only distinguished grammatically where this is necessary in order to avoid ambiguity. But the kind of generalization described above is very characteristic of the way languages work.

Mood

Another function of clause structure is to signal mood. Are we asking or telling? Are we talking about what is happening in our world, about what is not happening, about what we think may be happening, or about what we would like to happen? The simplest way of expressing such meanings is to add appropriate grammatical words. In English, for example, we can express uncertainty by saying 'perhaps' or 'possibly'. Japanese makes 'yes'/'no' questions by putting the particle *ka* (a sort of spoken question mark) at the end of the equivalent statement. French has a complex interrogative particle *est-ce que* ('is it that') which can be added to the beginning of an utterance. Less simply, the relevant meaning can be expressed by altering the verb or verb phrase, as in one form of Japanese negation: 'understand(s)' is *wakarimasu* and 'do(es) not understand' is *wakarimasen*. In other cases, the whole clause structure may be modified. An English 'yes'/'no' question can be marked by a rising intonation contour ('You're sure?'), most often with added verb–subject inversion ('She has phoned' → 'Has she phoned?') and frequently with an added auxiliary and further changes in the subject–verb complex ('She went' → 'Did she go?'). Auxiliaries are also used in English to express degrees of possibility and certainty ('Can we pay?', 'Your new job must be interesting').

Analysing phrases and clauses

A phrase like 'my old yellow sweater' is not simply a cluster of items from different word classes. One of the words—'sweater'—has a different status from the others. The phrase identifies a particular sweater, not a particular 'my' or 'old' or 'yellow'. There is a sense, therefore, in which 'sweater' is the core of the complex, with the other three words acting as satellites: it is the **head** of this particular noun phrase, and the other words are modifiers.

The three modifying words are not all of a kind. 'Old' and 'yellow' are adjectives: words which typically refer to qualities, and are used to define or describe. 'My', as we have seen, is rather different: possessives, along with articles and quantifiers like 'every', 'any', and 'many', belong to a class called **determiners**, which behave differently from adjectives, and whose function is largely to delimit the reference of nouns by showing what part of a general class is being talked about. One way of analysing a noun phrase like 'my old yellow sweater' is to regard the adjectives as modifying the noun, and the determiner as modifying the whole adjective-plus-noun complex. The tree diagram in Figure 2.1 shows this structure.

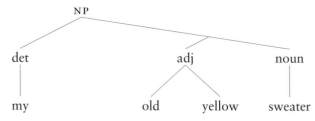

Figure 2.1

Clauses, like phrases, can be analysed into their constituents. It can be useful, in this kind of analysis, to distinguish form and function. From a formal point of view, for example, the expression 'my younger brother' is simply a noun phrase (NP); but from a functional point of view it may be a subject in one clause, an object in another, and something else in a third. Similarly, the adjective 'big' can function as a modifier in a NP in one context—'a big house'—and as the head of a free-standing adjective phrase in another—'the house is quite big'. Figure 2.2 shows one possible (rather simplified) way of analysing the clause 'my younger brother has bought a new house in the country'.

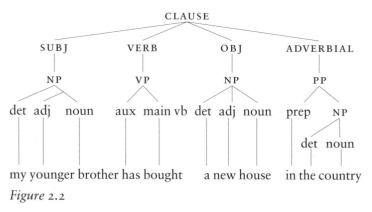

Figure 2.2

Clauses inside clauses

Participants in situations and events are not necessarily people or things. They can also be other situations or events, as when somebody loses her keys (situation A), and this situation causes problems (situation B). This kind of scenario may call for a more complex kind of grammatical structure than the simple NP–VP–NP subject–verb–object pattern. A common solution in English is to integrate two clauses, so that, for example, one clause takes on the role of subject, object, or complement in the other.

> *The fact that she had lost her keys* caused a problem.
> She told the police *that she had lost her keys*.
> The problem was *that she had lost her keys*.

The special status of one clause as a component of the other is marked in these examples by the conjunction 'that'.

Clauses can also function adverbially inside other clauses, giving information about time, place, cause, or any of the other possible relationships between two situations. The exact nature of the link may be marked by a specific conjunction.

> *After she had lost her keys* she went to the police.
> She went to the police *because she had lost her keys*.

A clause can be **embedded** in a noun phrase. When we particularize a noun, we may wish to do so not by listing its qualities, as in 'my old yellow sweater', but by referring to an event or situation which identifies it: 'the sweater that Auntie Lucy gave me'. Clauses that modify nouns in this way are called **relative clauses**; in English, their status is often marked by words such as 'that', 'which', or 'who'.

Full clauses in English are structured around so-called **finite verbs**, for example, 'goes', 'travelled', 'will play', whose meaning includes the expression of time relations. **Non-finite** forms like 'gone', 'to travel', 'playing' can also form the nuclei of clause-like structures which may be embedded inside other clauses.

> *To travel hopefully* is better than *to arrive*.
> I will never forget *playing in that match*.

Embedding does not stop, so to speak, one level down. Embedded clauses can have their own embedded clauses. This **recursion** is common in some written registers.

The fact that the woman who lives across the road had forgotten where she had put her keys after she had locked her house caused a problem that ultimately affected everyone who lived in the street.

English relative clauses lend themselves easily to recursion, as illustrated in the old nursery rhyme 'The house that Jack built'.

… This is the dog that worried the cat that killed the rat that ate the malt that lay in the house that Jack built.

The units of language

It has been convenient in this chapter to talk as if the basic units of language as code and message were words and phrases respectively. This is, however, a simplification. Many English words are composed of smaller meaningful elements, or **morphemes**: for example, 'work-ed', 'un-happi-ness'. In some languages, as we shall see, words in use can have very complex morphemic structures, to the point where the word–phrase distinction becomes obscured. (Even in English, this is not totally clear-cut: see Chapter 4.)

Higher-level structures can be divided into units in various ways, depending both on a grammarian's purpose and on his or her view of how language works. To take a simple example: in the sentence 'She went to the police because she had lost her keys', is the second clause necessarily an adverbial constituent of the first, as in the hierarchical analysis suggested earlier, or should it be seen instead as an independent clause linked by a conjunction, giving a 'flatter' analysis? (And does our answer to this question say something real about the sentence, or does it only reflect the conceptual framework that we are imposing on it?) Grammarians looking for a general theory which will account for the multifarious architectures of the world's languages make very different choices of basic units and structural principles, and these choices give rise to very different kinds of grammar. A linguistics encyclopaedia on my bookshelf contains references to 'cognitive grammar', 'relational grammar', 'word grammar', 'text grammar', 'head driven phrase structure grammar', 'generalized phrase structure grammar', 'Montague grammar', 'transformational grammar', 'dependency grammar', 'stratificational grammar', 'systemic grammar', and some twenty other models.

Despite their considerable differences, most grammatical theories come down on one side or the other of a fundamental divide, taking either formal units (for example, noun phrase) or functional units (for example, subject) as primary. **Formal** approaches (such as **generative grammar**, see Chapter 8) see **syntax** as more or less autonomous, organized in ways that cannot easily be accounted for by reference to meaning or function, but that reflect the structure of the human cognitive faculty, or the hypothesized language module that forms part of that faculty. **Functional** approaches, in contrast, account for the structure of language in terms of the functions it has to perform. This view holds, broadly, that any mental system whose purpose is to represent the world and enable its users to communicate messages by means of a serial code will necessarily have the structural characteristics that we observe in human language.

It is, of course, possible to adopt a compromise position: that grammar exists in order to make possible the communication of certain kinds of meaning, but that once in existence it takes on a life of its own, and that it therefore has both functional and autonomous features, corresponding not only to the jobs it has to do but also to the way human cognition is organized.

Whatever the truth of the matter, these disagreements clearly reflect the fact that the mechanisms of syntax, so limited and simple in principle, come to generate the highly complex structures that characterize language in practice. It is this complexity, daunting though it may sometimes seem, that helps to make possible the range and creativity of expression that typify human communication, and which, as we shall see in the next chapter, is realized in strikingly different ways in the world's languages.

3
Grammar in the world's languages

As we have seen, the mechanisms of grammar, simple though they are in principle, can develop considerable complexity. How much complexity, and of what kind, differs from one language to another. Languages vary greatly in the number of word classes they establish, in the extent to which they select word order, inflection, or function words for their basic grammatical purposes, and in the additional meanings which they choose to express by means of these devices. In this chapter we will look at some examples of these differences.

Word classes

For English speakers, it might seem self-evident that every language should have the familiar nine or so 'parts of speech' listed in their grammars. However, this is by no means the case. Nouns, verbs, adjectives, and adverbs are certainly more or less universal categories, but their membership varies significantly across languages, and neither adjectives nor adverbs are necessarily large open-ended classes as they are in English. Swahili adjectives constitute a closed group with fifty members; the Amazonian language Jarawara has fourteen; the Niger-Congo language Igbo has eight. The English closed classes of grammatical words are not at all universal: Australian languages generally have nothing that corresponds to English prepositions, while Carib languages have no conjunctions or relative pronouns.

This does not, of course, mean that these languages cannot handle the relevant concepts. Qualities can perfectly well be encoded as verbs or nouns. Some languages with limited adjective classes have verbs which translate into English as, for instance, 'to be high' or 'to be interesting'. In Hausa the idea of 'hard wood' is expressed by the equivalent of 'wood having hardness'; 'it is hard' by 'it is with hardness'. The notions expressed by English prepositions may be conveyed elsewhere by using verbs (as when we say in English 'facing' to mean 'opposite'), or in other ways: Finnish uses noun endings to express many spatio-temporal relationships. The South American language Quechua has **affixes** where English has personal pronouns:

Maqa-ma-nki
hit-me-you
(you hit me)

Many languages contain word classes which are exotic to an English eye. Tagalog has politeness markers—*po* and *ho*—which are added to sentences to indicate respect, as well as **mood** markers which label sentences as conveying wishes, speculation, or enquiry. Japanese has a range of postpositional particles which are added to nouns to express grammatical and discourse relations.

Kenji ga   Yoko ni sono hon o   watashita.
Kenji SUB Yoko IO that book DO gave.
(Kenji gave Yoko that book.)

Sono hito wa,   Nihonjin   desu ka?
That man TOP, (a) Japanese is   Q?
(Is that man Japanese?)

(SUB = subject particle; IO = indirect object particle;
DO = direct object particle; TOP = topicalization particle;
Q = interrogative particle)

Words used for counting constitute complex systems in some languages. Nivkh (spoken in the far east of the Asian continent) has twenty-six subsystems of cardinal numbers, used for counting different kinds of object. Such systems often involve the use of **classifiers** together with numbers. A Mandarin Chinese example:

na   liang-ben   shu
those two CLASSIFIER book
(those two   books)

The choice of classifier in such cases depends on the subclass of the following noun. So the Mandarin Chinese for 'two' is *liang-ben* if one is counting books, but *liang-zhang* if one is counting certain flat things like tables, maps, or papers, and *liang-jian* if one is counting events or some kinds of clothing; *liang-li* is used for granular things like grains of sand or rice; *liang-tiao* for items of news, snakes, and some other things. (We actually do something like this in English when we are partitioning mass nouns, for example, 'three blades of grass', 'three loaves of bread', 'three bars of soap', 'three grains of rice'.) Classifiers can be very numerous: Thai has over sixty.

The division of nouns into grammatically distinct subclasses or **genders** is found in many unrelated languages. African languages can have as many as twenty genders. Most Indo-European languages (modern English is a rare exception) assign nouns to two or three classes called, for instance, 'masculine', 'feminine', and 'neuter', each of which may require different versions of accompanying determiners, adjectives, and/or verb forms. A French example:

> *le   long rapport que j'ai   écrit*   (*rapport* is masculine)
> the long report   that I have written

> *la   longue lettre que j'ai   écrite*   (*lettre* is feminine)
> the long   letter that I have written

Although noun class divisions often have a partly **semantic** basis, as in Mandarin Chinese, membership tends to be largely arbitrary and unpredictable. This is particularly the case for Indo-European languages, despite the apparent implications of the terms 'masculine' and 'feminine'. In Spanish, hands and ears are feminine but feet and eyes are masculine. The French masculine sun and feminine moon have opposite-gender counterparts in German. The German words for 'knife', 'fork', and 'spoon' are neuter, feminine, and masculine respectively. Words for male entities do tend to be masculine, and their female counterparts feminine, but even here gender assignment is rather hit-and-miss: the French for 'sentry'—usually a masculine role—is the feminine noun *sentinelle*, while the German for 'girl', *Mädchen*, is neuter.

Structural types

Languages can be distinguished and classified by reference to what kind of grammar they prefer. A traditional approach takes **morphology**, or word structure, as a basis. In so-called **isolating** or 'analytic' languages like Vietnamese or Chinese, words do not change their forms at all; grammatical relations are shown by word order and the use of function words. In **inflecting** or 'synthetic' languages like Russian or Greek, on the other hand, words take on different forms in order to indicate their grammatical status. **Agglutinating** languages like Turkish or Navajo go to extremes in this direction, with words incorporating whole sequences of morphemes: the Turkish for 'to our cars' is *araba-lar-ımız-a* ('car' + plural + **first-person** plural + dative).

In this framework, English comes towards the isolating end of the scale. Its ancestor Anglo-Saxon was a morphologically complex language in which nouns, pronouns, adjectives, and verbs had numerous possible forms. Modern English has traded in most of its grammatical inflections for word order and the use of function words. All that remains is the possessive noun inflection (for example, 'brother's'), half a dozen distinct subject and object forms (for example, 'I'/'me', 'they'/'them', etc.), the fossil **third-person** singular present '-s' as in 'says', a few other verb inflections ('-ing', '-ed', and some irregular forms), and the comparison endings '-er' and '-est'. English does, however, have substantial **derivational morphology**—affixes such as 'un-', 'anti-', '-ness', '-ation', '-ize', or '-ly', which add **lexical** meanings or alter word class rather than showing grammatical relations.

Although this approach to classification is useful as a generalization, languages do not necessarily fit neatly into one or other category. Japanese, for example, is isolating in some ways and agglutinating in others. Nouns do not inflect, and functions such as subject or object are shown by the particles referred to above: *hito ga* means 'man subject', while *hito o* is 'man object'. On the other hand, Japanese verbs do inflect and can express a wide variety of meanings morphologically. Another problem with this kind of general classification is that it is not very informative. Grouping languages into 'isolating', 'agglutinating', and 'inflecting' does not necessarily reveal relationships between them, or lead to useful generalizations. Contemporary typological approaches concentrate on describing and comparing more specific features across languages, such as number and type of word classes, phrase structure, pronoun systems, clause structure, agreement systems, and word-order preferences.

Morphological complexity

A Russian who wants to produce the English phrase 'in my garden' needs to know those three words—nothing more. In contrast, an English speaker who tries to construct the Russian equivalent, *v moyom sadu*, finds the garden turning into a grammatical jungle:

- Singular Russian nouns have up to six distinct 'case' forms: nominative, accusative, genitive, dative, prepositional, and instrumental. These correspond to different grammatical functions of the noun, and are differentiated by word endings (inflections).
- The Russian for 'in', *v*, is followed by the prepositional case. (Other prepositions may be followed by the accusative, genitive, dative, or instrumental.)
- Russian nouns come in different classes with various sets of case inflections.
- The Russian for 'garden', *sad*, belongs to the so-called 'masculine' class, and to that subclass whose prepositional singular ends in a stressed '-e'.
- *Sad*, however, is exceptional: after the preposition *v*, *sadu* is used instead of *sade*.
- The Russian for 'my' has nine singular forms. To agree in both gender and case with *sadu*, the masculine prepositional form *moyem* is required.

Adding an adjective would introduce a whole new dimension of complication.

Inflecting languages do not have a monopoly on complexity, as Russians find, for example, when they grapple with the innocuous-looking English function words 'the' and 'a'/'an'. These have no equivalent in Russian (or in most of the world's languages), and their meanings and distribution are so hard to analyse and learn that few non-native speakers of English completely master their use. However, in inflecting languages morphology often seems to take on a life of its own, reaching levels of elaboration that go well beyond the functional basis for its existence.

The Russian pattern illustrated is typical of the present or past states of many Indo-European languages. European schoolchildren once had to memorize tables of the endings belonging to the various Latin **declensions** (noun and adjective classes) and **conjugations** (verb classes), with their numerous subclasses and exceptions. While the modern descendants of Latin have lost most of their noun endings, they have retained considerable verbal complexity: a typical Spanish verb can have up to 110 different forms, including compounds formed with auxiliaries.

Inflections can have various functions. Latin verb forms gave information about **person** (speaker, hearer, or 'third person'), **number** (singular or plural), **tense** (time relations), **mood** (whether reference was to established facts or not), and **voice** (active or passive). Nouns inflected for number and case, distinguishing subject, **direct object/indirect object**, and possessive relationships; different prepositions were also followed by different cases (see Table 3.1).

Caesar (a singular, masculine, third-declension noun):
cases and typical functions

FORM	CASE	FUNCTION	EXAMPLE
Caesar	nominative	subject	*Caesar Galliam vicit.* (Caesar conquered Gaul.)
Caesarem	accusative	direct object	*Brutus Caesarem interfecit.* (Brutus killed Caesar.)
Caesaris	genitive	possession	*Equus Caesaris.* (Caesar's horse.)
Caesari	dative	indirect object	*Id redde Caesari.* (Give this to Caesar.)
Caesare	ablative	other	*a Caesare* (by/from Caesar)

Table 3.1

Details of case grammar differ considerably from one language to another. In the North American language Kawaiisu, for example, the subjects of negative sentences are accusative. And in many languages the subjects of **intransitive** verbs have the same form as the objects of transitive verbs.

A characteristic of many inflecting languages is the way several functions coalesce in one inflection. In the German sentence *Mein Vater hat einen grossen Hund* ('My father has a big dog'), for instance, the *-en* at the end of *einen* indicates simultaneously that the following noun is a direct object, singular, and a member of the so-called masculine noun class. As a result of phonetic changes, modern German has relatively few distinct inflections, so a particular form may also be found in several environments. Attached to a different kind of word in a different context, *-en* might signal plural, genitive singular, dative singular, first/second/third person plural (of a verb), infinitive, or past participle.

Morphological marking does not only operate through suffixes, as in the examples above. Prefixes and infixes are used in many languages. The body of a word may also be partly or completely changed, as in English 'foot'/'feet', 'bring'/'brought', 'go'/'went', or 'be'/'am'/'is'/'was'. In Welsh the initial sound of a word can change ('soft mutation'): the word for 'tooth', for example, is *dant*, *ddant*, or *nhant*, depending on its context and grammatical function. Bambara, like many African languages, uses tone. A low final tone on a noun expresses **definiteness**: 'coffee' is *káfé*, while 'the coffee' is *káfè*.

Where numerous functions are realized morphologically, as in agglutinating languages, words can have massively complex structures with hundreds or even thousands of possible forms. Verbs in many Native American languages have structures involving a fixed order of positions for various classes of affix, each expressing a different grammatical or semantic element. Navajo has prefix positions for: (1) indirect object/reflexive; (2) repetitive marker; (3) plural marker; (4) direct object; (5) demonstrative; (6) adverbial morphemes; (7) mode/**aspect** marker; (8) subject marker; (9) classifier. Jarawara has three prefix and twenty-five suffix positions. This type of structure can blur the distinction between words, phrases, and clauses. In the Australian language Murrinh-Patha, for example, object nouns can be incorporated into verbs: 'he will cut his hand' is *putmartalnu* ('he-hand-cut-will'). Ket, spoken in Siberia, can incorporate objects, intransitive subjects, instruments, and directional adverbs into the verb. The Canadian language Nootka uses one word for 'He invites people to a feast'.

Agreement

Morphological signalling of grammatical relations frequently goes beyond individual words to involve **agreement**, whereby the form of one word is determined by the form or grammatical class of another. The components of noun phrases are often linked in this way. Agreement marking may be relatively opaque: while a Russian speaker knows implicitly that the words *moyom sadu* belong together because of their form, the two masculine singular prepositional endings have nothing overtly in common. Italian noun phrase morphology is partially transparent: 'white wine' is *vino bianco*, while 'a white house' is *una casa bianca*. On the other hand, in *una questione difficile* ('a difficult question') and *un esame difficile* ('a difficult exam'), the difference of noun class is unmarked except by the choice of article. At the most transparent extreme, many Bantu languages have prefixes showing noun-class membership which are repeated throughout the noun phrase. A Swahili example:

ki-kapu ki-kubwa ki-moja
basket   large   one
(one large basket)

Participant roles such as subject or object can be marked by noun–verb agreement. In Indo-European languages verb forms commonly reflect the number and person of their subjects. There are vestiges of this in English in the forms of 'to be' ('am'/'are'/'is'/ 'was'/'were'), and in the third-person singular present '-s' inflection (for example, 'works', 'sits'). In many languages, indeed, the grammatical subject can be identified when necessary not by its form or position, but purely by the form of the verb: the verb carries an inflection which indicates that, of the candidate nouns, the subject is the one belonging to a particular semantic or formal class. (As if in English we distinguished 'The car hit the boulder' from 'The boulder hit the car' by saying in one case 'Car boulder moving-thing-hit' and in the other 'Car boulder round-thing-hit'.) An example from Mohawk:

> *Ieksá:'a raksá:'a wahonwá:'ienhte'*
> girl   boy   hit
> (The girl hit the boy.)

> *Ieksá:'a raksá:'a wahshakó:ienhte'*
> girl   boy   hit
> (The boy hit the girl.)

In other languages, it is the object rather than the subject which is marked on the verb; and in yet other cases, as we have seen, the verb has several 'slots' which can be filled by affixes identifying the subject, direct and indirect object, and/or other types of participant.

Agreement can involve other syntactic elements besides noun phrases and verbs—for instance, adverbs. This may sound exotic to English speakers, but we do not have to look far from home for an illustration. In many English **dialects**, as in Romance languages, negative verbs are accompanied by corresponding negative forms of adverbs and pronouns. An American song by Bert Williams contains the line: 'I ain't never done nothing to nobody, and I ain't never got nothing from nobody no time'.

Meanings

A tool developed for one purpose often turns out to have other uses. Computers started out as superior calculating machines: today few people use them to add or multiply, but we depend on them in innumerable other ways. A similar functional explosion characterizes the devices that we call 'grammar'. As I suggested in Chapter 1, these devices are perhaps strictly essential only for a limited range of purposes which cannot be handled by vocabulary alone: identifying participant roles, marking structural relations, and indicating the modal status of utterances. In practice, however, they turn out to be convenient and economical vehicles for the expression of a great variety of other concepts and relationships.

In English alone, grammatical features can express time relations, verbal aspect (**perfective**/non-perfective, **progressive**/non-progressive), number, definiteness, person, sex, and **animacy**; they can distinguish between discrete entities like cats and non-discrete entities like air, perfume, or dust; and they can convey very many other meanings that English speakers or their remote ancestors have chosen to encode in the grammatical core of their language.

Many of these concepts, for instance, person, sex, animacy, time relations, and number, appear frequently in the grammar of the world's languages. (Details naturally vary—for instance, the expression of time relations and event types differs greatly from one language to another; and number systems can involve not only a singular/plural division, but also distinct dual, trial, or paucal forms to refer to two, three, or an unspecified small number of entities.) However, **grammaticalization** of these meanings is certainly not universal. English speakers are often surprised to discover that many languages manage perfectly well without putting either time or number into the grammar—if it is necessary to be precise about these things, extra words can be added (on the lines of 'Two man phone last night'). At the same time, languages worldwide express various meanings which English sees no need to grammaticalize. Some Native American and Australian languages have a 'visibility' category: the form of nouns and pronouns shows whether speakers can see the things they are referring to at the moment of speaking. In the many languages which encode **evidentiality**, verb forms must show how speakers have gained the knowledge they are communicating, for example, as eyewitnesses, by hearsay, through common knowledge, or through inference. There are two kinds of third-person pronoun in some Native American languages: one to refer to the person or entity that is the centre of attention, and a different one for others. Numerous languages have two equivalents of 'we', depending on whether the reference includes the hearer or not. A distinction between **alienable possession** and **inalienable possession** is common, with 'I have three brothers', for instance, being expressed by a different structure from 'I have a car'. Far Eastern languages such as Korean or Javanese are among those that have very elaborate grammatical devices for showing respect and relative social status.

Because grammar expresses meanings which are fundamental to our perceptions of the world, it offers great metaphorical potential. English uses temporal distance to symbolize other kinds of detachment or remoteness. A question or request can be made less direct, and therefore more polite, by locating it grammatically in the past or future: 'Who did you wish to speak to?'; 'I was wondering if ...'; 'That'll be £3.50'; 'I'll just get you to sign in'. Spatial distance can stand in for affective distance: we say 'I like *this* music, what is it?' but 'Turn off *that* bloody noise'. Many languages use pronouns metaphorically to imply respect. To address a single hearer by a plural pronoun (such as French *vous*) symbolically gives him or her increased importance; a third-person pronoun suggests a respectfully indirect approach.

Since different languages encode very different kinds of meaning in their grammars, it is natural to ask whether their speakers perceive or categorize reality differently. This old idea that our language shapes the way we think—**linguistic relativity**—was given new impetus in the early twentieth century, as anthropologists and linguists amassed more detailed knowledge about the world's languages. It was observed that the North American language Hopi, for instance, grammaticalizes time quite differently from European languages; this led linguists such as Edward Sapir and Benjamin Lee Whorf to suggest that Hopi and English speakers might also conceptualize time in quite different ways. The Sapir-Whorf hypothesis was not well supported by subsequent research, and it fell into disfavour as belief in 'universal grammar' gained strength (see Chapter 8). However, interest in the view has revived recently, and researchers investigating links between language and cognition are finding evidence that certain forms of linguistic relativity may indeed exist.

Why is everything so complicated?

Looking at the world's grammatical systems, it is hard to avoid bewilderment. Why is everything so complicated? What is it all for? A Russian speaker could obviously express the notion of 'my' perfectly well without having to choose between nine singular and four plural forms in accordance with arcane rules of number, gender, and case morphology. Counting in Chinese is not obviously facilitated by adding the appropriate noun classifier after every number. Why do English speakers have to select from six subtly differentiated tense/aspect forms every time they want to talk about past events, whether or not this contributes anything useful? What is the value of forcing Navajo speakers to adapt every verb in order to indicate the source of their information? In any case, these systems are not necessarily very efficient: German has six forms of the word for 'good', but *guter* is still ambiguous between nominative masculine singular, genitive feminine singular, and genitive plural. It is easy to feel, as did the inventors of artificial languages such as Esperanto, that with a little thought one could easily devise a much better system.

One of the factors contributing to linguistic complexity is history. As languages develop, phonetic changes alter and erode words, so that regular and predictable sets of forms can change into collections of idiosyncratic and unpredictable endings. Linguistic features outlive their use: morphological case-marking does not necessarily disappear completely when word order takes over its function. The consequence is that all languages have their grammatical junk-rooms containing worn-out apparatus and old-fashioned tools that have been replaced. It may be, however, that the retention of older linguistic signalling devices alongside new ones is advantageous: such redundancy renders communication more resistant to breakdown.

Another factor is the apparent human tendency to make rules and systems apply universally. In newly-developed **creoles**, the expression of time relations has been observed to move progressively from optional to obligatory over a few generations. It is not entirely clear why this should be so, but perhaps less computational effort is required to obey a rule all the time than to work out on each occasion whether one needs to or not. (As when we stop automatically at a red light whether or not there seems to be any other traffic around.)

A third element is the fact that speakers of a language have little incentive to tidy it up, because its complexities cause them no difficulty. Children succeed, completely unconsciously, in achieving mastery of extraordinarily elaborate linguistic systems. The West African language Fula has taken morphology to the point where each word virtually has its own idiosyncratic set of inflections; although these take time to master, adult Fula speakers have no more trouble with their system than English speakers have with the formation of English noun plurals. Not only do language users live happily with complexity: they actually seem to generate it. (A study of children using Esperanto has found that they introduced irregularities into this totally regular language!) Perhaps, as is sometimes suggested, making one's own language difficult acts as a barrier to outsiders, and consequently as a badge of membership: if only the children of the tribe can learn it, you know who your own people are.

4

Grammar and vocabulary

How different are grammar and vocabulary?

Students of languages learn both vocabulary items (for example, *vert* is the French for 'green'; *arbre* means 'tree') and grammatical **rules** (French adjectives follow nouns, so 'a green tree' is *un arbre vert*). It seems obvious—at least, if we look at languages like French or English—that these are quite different kinds of thing. Vocabulary (we might say if we were explaining it to a child) is words; grammar is to do with putting words together. Vocabulary consists of specific items—the things we find in a dictionary. Grammar seems to have a more general character, involving rules that apply to whole categories of items.

Many grammatical rules do, indeed, have a very general scope. They may describe the way one category of word relates to another, as with French noun–adjective order, or the fact that English prepositions are followed by '-ing' forms of verbs ('without paying'; 'on leaving'). The focus of a rule may itself be a grammatical structure, taking grammar still further away from vocabulary—for example, the position of Japanese relative clauses, or the use of the English present progressive to describe ongoing activity as in 'I'm reading'. Other grammatical rules, however, are more closely attached to **lexis**. Many languages, for instance, show certain kinds of grammatical meaning morphologically, by changes in the form of words. Not only can these inflectional systems be very complex; they can also involve different sets of inflections for different subclasses of words, as students of such languages know to their cost. While, for example, the third person singular future active form of the Latin verb *amare* ('to love') is *amabit*, the corresponding form of *regere* ('to rule') is not *regebit* but *reget*, because the two verbs belong to different subclasses or 'conjugations'. Subclasses can be quite restricted. The morphology and syntax of English **modal auxiliaries**, for example, relate mainly to just ten verbs: 'can', 'could', 'may', 'might', 'will', 'would', 'shall', 'should', 'must', and 'ought'. Croatian *braća* ('brothers') is one of a very few plural nouns in that language which are feminine singular in form, and are used with feminine singular adjectives but plural verbs. At this point, grammar comes very close to vocabulary.

The grammar of words

The closeness is even more apparent if we approach the question from the other end, so to speak—if, instead of looking at rules and their scope, we consider individual words and their grammatical characteristics. A typical entry in our mental lexicon may include a great deal of structural information alongside specifications of meaning and use. To begin with, words belong to grammatical classes. *Arbre* not only means 'tree'; it is a noun, and therefore behaves differently from French verbs, adjectives, or other types of word. It is also a particular kind of noun: it is countable, and therefore has a distinct plural form *arbres*; and as a member of the 'masculine' subclass, it is used with the articles *un* and *le*, not *une* and *la*. Class membership may be signalled overtly by form: an Italian word ending in *-mente*, for example, is likely to be an adverb of manner; most English words ending in '-ation' are nouns derived from verbs. The grammar associated with word classes may be very complex: verbs in some languages can have dozens or even hundreds of forms expressing, for example, distinctions of person, number, tense, and mood.

Word grammar is not simply a function of the class that a word belongs to. A word can have its own unique grammatical profile. This is often the case for irregular forms, which may constitute, so to speak, a class of one, like English 'penny' with its plural 'pence', or 'lose' with its past form 'lost'. Syntax, as well as morphology, can be specific to a word. The English verb 'suggest' can be followed by an '-ing' form ('I suggest leaving now') but not an infinitive (*'I suggest to leave now'); the converse is true of 'expect'. 'Rely' needs a preposition before an object ('I can rely on you'); 'trust' does not ('I can trust you'). English past participles, unlike adjectives, are not normally modified by 'very' (compare 'much loved' and 'very popular'); but there are word-specific exceptions: we say 'very annoyed'. Indeed, it is becoming clear from research on large language databases (or 'corpora') that every word in a language is involved in a complex and unique network of patterns and relationships. Some of these relationships are unambiguously grammatical, like part-of-speech membership. Some are purely **lexical**, like **collocational** restrictions: we can say 'sharply different' or 'slightly different', but we are less likely to say 'highly different' or 'mildly different'; we say 'a blazing row' or 'a flaming row' but not normally 'a burning row'. In between these extremes, however, there is a large middle ground where grammar and lexis interact, and where the dividing line is far from clear.

On the frontier

Words, then, may contain a lot of grammar. In some languages, indeed, so much overt grammatical information is packaged inside individual words that the distinction between grammar and vocabulary comes close to breaking down. The single Turkish word *öpüştürüldüler*, for example, corresponds to English 'they were caused to kiss each other'; Finnish *autostammekin* means 'from our car, too'.

It is not only morphologically complex words that straddle the frontier between grammar and vocabulary. As we have seen, languages also have simple lexical items whose main function is to manage the internal affairs of the language, rather than to refer to elements in the outside world. English uses forms of the auxiliary verb 'do' to construct questions and negatives. The Thai word *máy* makes a sentence interrogative. Japanese adds various short words to nouns to show their grammatical status as **topic**, subject, object, or possessor. These particles are not really very different from morphological inflections: compare Japanese *hon o* ('book' + object particle) with the Russian equivalent *knigu* ('book-' + object inflection).

Some of these function words have little or no referential meaning: their function is simply the grammatical purpose that they serve. (It would be pointless to ask what 'do' means in 'Do you know where Peter is?') Others occupy more of the middle ground between grammar and vocabulary. Prepositions are often regarded as 'grammar', but most of them can be used to convey clear lexical meanings to do with temporal or spatial relationships (for example, 'after', 'under', 'at', 'with'). On the other hand, these meanings are often **bleached** out in particular contexts ('look after', 'under these circumstances', 'at least', 'cope with'). This bleaching, where words lose their lexical meaning and take on purely grammatical functions, is a common process in language development (see Chapter 6), and is another factor in the blurring of the distinction between vocabulary and grammar.

Language in use: chunking

The distinction becomes even more unclear if we look at language in actual use rather than in terms of a conventional grammatical analysis. From a purely analytic point of view, words are names for particular categories—'car', 'buy', and 'new', for example, refer to classes of thing, action, and quality respectively—while grammar helps to turn strings of words into structures that convey specific messages: 'I've bought a new car'. But there are messages and messages. Some are certainly unique, one-offs: 'There's a dead rat on the top shelf behind grandma's ice-axe'. Other messages, though, are recurrent, corresponding to the many familiar types of situation and event in our lives, and these are likely to be repeated whenever appropriate: 'Sorry I'm late'; 'Thanks a lot'; 'I think so'; 'I'd like a receipt'; 'as much as possible'; 'Can I look round?'. In a sense, these everyday recurrent messages could almost be regarded as long words. Like single words, they have a 'class' character, relating to familiar categories of experience: apologizing for being late, expressing gratitude, expressing cautious agreement, asking for a receipt, talking about the maximum that is practicable, explaining that one does not immediately want to buy something. And, according to psycholinguists, they are likely to be handled mentally in the same way as words. When we say 'Sorry I'm late', we almost certainly do not select the separate words and perform the various operations (more complex than they may appear) that are necessary to combine the words into a grammatically, situationally, and stylistically correct and appropriate English sentence. Most probably, we recall the expression as a whole from our store of useful prefabricated formulae. Seen from this point of view, 'Sorry I'm late' is really no more complex, in actual use, than 'Sorry': it is simply a longer word which happens to have spaces in it if we write it down.

Formulaic language of this kind, often called 'chunks', has attracted substantial research in recent years, especially since the growth of large electronic corpora has made it easier to tabulate the fixed or semi-fixed combinations that words typically enter into. It has become clear that languages contain very large numbers of such multi-word items: one often-quoted estimate suggests that English, for example, may have hundreds of thousands. If this seems hard to believe, think how many common fixed expressions are built around the noun 'work': 'at work', 'work in progress', 'go to work', 'a day's work', 'man's'/'woman's work', 'take pride in one's work', 'part-time work', 'shift work', 'the world of work', 'nice work', 'carry out work', 'in the course of one's work', 'out of work', 'build on somebody's work', 'work permit', 'take work home', 'equal pay for equal work', 'the work of a moment', 'look for work', 'all my own work', and so on. One can easily think of dozens more, and this is only one meaning of one noun.

Many such expressions constitute what one might call **selectional idioms**: our conventionally preferred ways of expressing frequently-occurring meanings. There are many possible options, for example, for apologizing in English for keeping somebody waiting. We could perfectly well say 'I'm sorry I made you wait'; 'I'm sorry I caused you to wait'; 'I apologize because you had to wait'; 'Forgive me for the delay'. But it happens that we normally say '(I'm) sorry to keep you waiting': this expression is a part of idiomatic English in a way that the others are not. Selectional idioms of this kind occur in all languages, and they cause serious problems for those foreign learners who aim to approach native-speaker competence. Such learners not only have to know the grammar and vocabulary of the language they are studying, but also a whole inventory of preferred formulae corresponding to the most common recurrent meanings and situations. Paradoxically, it may be easier, with an intermediate knowledge of a language, to produce novel one-off utterances correctly than conventional everyday expressions. Basic grammar and vocabulary will allow you to say that you saw a strange bird in the tree across the road yesterday, but they will not help you to produce the normal equivalent of 'I'm being served': as with individual words, if you do not know the appropriate form, you cannot invent it.

Our repertoire of multi-word formulae includes many items which, despite their semi-lexical character, we would normally consider to be prototypically grammatical. When somebody says, for example, 'I'm going to start exercising regularly', they will probably not build the structure 'I'm going to' from scratch. It seems much more likely that this is recalled from store as a single chunk, as if it was a one-word future auxiliary. The normal pronunciation supports this interpretation: unless we are speaking slowly and carefully, we are likely to say not /aɪm gəʊɪŋ tuː/, but something more like /aŋnə/ or /amnə/. This 'chunk' character may obtain for very many of the common grammatical building blocks and frames which we use to construct our sentences, such as the English structures 'If I were you …'; 'What I meant was …'; 'she's been …-ing'; 'it would be … if …'; 'the most … in the …'; 'before we …, we'll need to …'; and so on.

Given the high frequency of many such lexicalized structures, and the size of the formulaic lexicon in general, it seems likely that prefabricated chunks of language will make up a large proportion of what is said and written in all languages. One study found that, of all verb + direct object combinations in a sample of English journalistic prose, between 37.5 per cent and 46 per cent could be classified as restricted collocations or idioms. Estimates of the amount of formulaic material in ordinary English **usage** range up to 80 per cent. Problems of definition and sampling make it impossible to establish a reliable figure, but the overall conclusion is inescapable: much of what we say and write falls into a category where vocabulary and grammar merge into each other.

A continuum

Rather than seeing grammar and vocabulary as totally separate and distinct, then, linguists are tending more and more to think in terms of a continuum. At one end there are facts about language that are indisputably lexical: *arbre* means 'tree'. At the other, there are phenomena that are purely grammatical: English relative clauses follow the noun phrases that they modify. In between the two extremes, there is the grammar of individual words; there are words that are as much grammar as vocabulary; there are structures that are bound to small groups of words; and there are structures that, in use at least, are more like vocabulary than grammar. As with most elements in the world that seem at first sight easy to distinguish, vocabulary and grammar are undoubtedly different kinds of thing, but there is no place where we can say 'This is where one stops and the other starts'.

5
Grammar in spoken and written text

Speech and writing

In a literate society, where writing is the principal vehicle of cultural transmission, and where behaviour is regulated by written documents such as laws and scriptures, the written word acquires great prestige. A society's language comes to be equated with its written form, and grammars are based on the analysis of written texts. Speech, whose evanescent structures are less open to inspection, is easily regarded as a poor relation of writing, conforming imperfectly to established grammatical norms. It is only recently, with our increased reliance on oral media and our greater ability to record and analyse speech, that we have found it easy to assess spoken language as a linguistic entity in its own right.

To talk about 'written' or 'spoken' language is, of course, to generalize over diverse types of communication with very varied stylistic characteristics. Prototypically, however, writing and speech are produced and interpreted under quite different circumstances. Most speech is interactive: conversational texts are constructed by speakers and listeners together as they exchange speaking turns, interrupt, interpolate responses, monitor each other's contributions, add clarifications and elaborations as necessary, and complete each other's utterances. Writing is a monologue, and a writer receives no immediate feedback. Clarity of structure and expression is consequently especially important in writing, since any confusion or ambiguity in a written text will remain unresolved. In view of these factors, together with the differences in communicative resources provided by the physical media of speech and writing, it is scarcely surprising that the two types of language should each have their own distinct grammatical characteristics.

Building phrases, clauses, and utterances

Writers can pause, reflect at length, recast, and revise, producing if they wish material with a high level of complexity. Speakers, composing online, are limited by working memory capacity in their ability to build up and keep track of elaborate structures. Equally, readers are far better able than listeners to decode complex material: one can read as slowly as one likes, backtracking as necessary, but one cannot listen at one's own speed.

Because of this, writing tends towards 'architectural' structuring, with relatively dense packaging of information, while speech favours more linear, chained structures, with information-bearing elements more spaced out. Written noun phrases (NPs) can become very elaborate, with determiners, adjectives, nouns, and postmodifying structures all clustering round a head noun. Spoken NPs generally contain few modifiers; subjects most often consist of a single pronoun. Writing often **nominalizes** elements which in speech would be expressed in separate clauses or other sequences.

- Writing: 'Peter's failure to gain a degree, and his subsequent refusal to look for work, caused his parents considerable concern.'
- Speech: 'Peter, you know, he didn't get a degree, and then he wouldn't do anything about getting a job, and of course, his parents, they got really worried.'

Written sentences vary enormously in length and complexity; at the upper limit they can exhibit elaborate **hierarchical organization** with complex embedding. Such elaboration is less common in speech. The average spoken clause length is around seven words; in formal writing the average can be double this. Speech, in fact, is not easily analysed into sentences; it is often better seen as constructed out of linear sequences of phrases and clauses, which are loosely linked into utterances in an add-on fashion rather than organized into structural hierarchies.

'And erm the thing is, I've gotta go to Cambridge on Friday, and Jane, I think she's out all day, because of the inspection.'
'Right.'
'So there's nobody here, so if you could, if you could come in for a couple of hours, in case the gas people come.'
'OK.'
'And then maybe you could pick Pauline up from school, which would really help, you know.'

Reference and context

For analytical purposes, it is often convenient to look at language on a small scale, as it is manifested in sentences, clauses, or phrases. However, language typically comes in more substantial stretches: for instance, a conversation, a song, a speech, an advertisement, a letter, an application form, a Parliamentary bill, a poem, or a novel. Such texts, whether spoken or written, need to be structured if they are to communicate successfully, and there are consequently aspects of grammar which relate principally to these larger units of language.

In constructing text, one important need is to manage reference. Having referred once to a particular person or thing—Red Riding Hood, the Conservative Party Conference, one's new washing machine, one's job, or whatever it may be—one may well want to do so again. It is not, however, economical to keep repeating the reference in the same form: 'One day Little Red Riding Hood decided to take some goodies to Little Red Riding Hood's grandmother. Little Red Riding Hood set off through the forest ...'. While languages vary in the extent to which they tolerate lexical repetition, there is a widespread tendency to handle repeated reference by using **anaphoric** (back-referring) pronouns: words with meanings in the area of 'that man/woman/person/thing that we are talking about'. The gain in economy from the use of such forms is necessarily offset by a loss of precision, so there is a certain potential for ambiguity: 'Ann told Beatrice she had made a bad mistake'. The potential is somewhat greater in languages which have only one pronoun corresponding to English 'he', 'she', and 'it'; less so in languages which have a large number of noun classes with distinct pronouns referring to them. In general, however, such ambiguities are easily avoided or resolved.

Other elements besides noun phrases can, of course, be recapitulated by **pro-forms**. English has words that substitute, for example, for previously-mentioned verbs ('I've already *done* it'), adjectives or relative clauses ('We would oppose *such* a decision'), and object clauses ('I hope *so*').

It may be unnecessary to make reference explicit. Where material has been stated before and can be predicted from the linguistic context, **ellipsis** is more economical: elements or parts of elements can simply be left out.

'She made every effort to comply, but in the end she was unable to (comply).'

'He was unwilling to approach the police, but he finally realized that he must (approach the police).'

'Why did you do that?'
'(I did that) To annoy you.'

Reference operates rather differently in writing and speech. Most writers are composing for unknown readers, and they cannot take shared context and knowledge for granted. Writing consequently tends to have more nouns and fewer pronouns than speech; pronoun reference is likely to be mainly internal, to previous parts of the text. Speech, in contrast, is characteristically anchored in the here and now. The context of conversation, consisting of the physical surroundings of the speakers, their shared knowledge, and the developing verbal exchange, may contain a good deal of information which does not have to be spelt out. Demonstratives are naturally more common in speech: 'Look at that!' Speech also has more substitute words like 'one', 'do', and 'so' which refer to the physical or spoken context: 'I'll take the blue ones'; 'She can't do it'; 'So were we!' Ellipsis is very common in casual conversation, with the situational context supplying the missing elements: 'Can't come in here'; 'Waiting for somebody?'; 'I don't think I can'; 'We don't want to'; 'If you like'; 'When you're ready'; 'Because I said so'; 'Why?' One speaker's 'incomplete' utterance may of course be part of a more complete two-speaker utterance:

'I didn't think you'd —'

'Want to stay. No, you're quite right.'

'Given' and 'new': information flow and topic-maintenance

Texts are built up incrementally, by integrating **new** information with old, **given** material. Consequently, it can be important to make the informational status of an element explicit: is the reference to something known or previously mentioned, or is something new being introduced? One function of the complex English article system is to indicate 'definiteness': to show whether or not a person or thing referred to is identifiable, known to both speaker/writer and hearer/reader. The sentence 'The woman started to sing', occurring in a text, is clearly marked by the article 'the' as referring to a woman who is identifiable, for example by virtue of already having been talked about; while 'A woman started to sing' equally clearly refers to someone who is not identifiable in the same way.

Languages (of which there are many) without definite articles or the inflectional equivalent naturally cannot indicate definiteness in this way. However, the distinction between given and new information can also be shown by ordering. Text tends to be organized on a given-new basis: sentences or clauses begin with what is known or can be taken for granted, leaving the main information focus until the end. Many languages handle this requirement by grammaticalizing a topic–comment structure, in which the given topic, which is not necessarily the subject, is announced separately at the beginning of a clause. This can give sentences on the lines of, for example, 'That lecture, I thought I was going to die of boredom'. English, especially written English, prefers to merge the topic with the grammatical subject, which is generally the first noun phrase in a clause. English subjects, accordingly, are far more likely to be grammatically definite (and thus referring to known entities) than indefinite. Indefinite subjects are often postponed—we say 'There's a man standing in the garden' rather than 'A man is standing in the garden'.

Merging topic and subject is unproblematic if the person or thing that is the topic is also the agent or principal participant in the action or situation that is being talked about; in that case the two categories naturally fall together. In other cases, some lexical or syntactic juggling may be required in order to choose verbs or structures that keep the topic in the subject slot. English is quite rich in pairs of verbs that facilitate this kind of manoeuvre: for example, 'like'/'please', 'admire'/'impress', 'frighten'/'fear', 'notice'/'strike', 'teach'/'learn'.

> 'All the staff *noticed* a certain change in her behaviour.'
> ('All the staff' is the topic.)

> 'The change in her behaviour *struck* all the staff quite forcibly.'
> ('The change' is the topic.)

Topic-maintenance is also a key reason for switching from active to passive and back.

> 'He *waited* for two hours; then he *was seen* by a doctor; then he *was sent* back to the waiting room. He *sat* there for another two hours—by this time he *was getting* angry. Then he *was taken* upstairs and *examined* by a specialist, after which he *had to* wait for another hour before he *was allowed* to go home.'

In spoken English, topic and subject are more often detached. Various kinds of topic-comment structure (some of which are called 'left-dislocation' by grammarians) make it possible to feed in parts of a message one at a time, giving a listener more time to process what is being said.

> 'This guy who rang up, he said ...'

> 'Those bloody bells, I didn't get a wink of sleep.'

> 'Last Wednesday it was, I was just going to work, ...'

> 'You know that necklace I bought. Well, I was putting it on yesterday ...'

Information (either new or given) can also be spaced out by putting some of it after a clause.

> 'I've got a new contract, I mean, just for a month, over in Dublin.'

> 'They work very hard, most of them.'

> 'She's pretty bright, that kid.'

The substance of speech—sound—can be manipulated in subtle and complex ways to structure text. In many languages, including English, **intonation** can show which parts of utterances are regarded as being background, given, common-ground material, and which parts carry the information focus. Given material in a clause typically has some kind of rising intonation contour, indicating incompleteness—there is something still to come—while the new information that is added is more likely to carry a falling contour, indicating completion. This helps to make speech less dependent than writing on ordering.

Phonological features can also be used to signal special focus or emphasis. A sentence like 'She only played tennis with Mr Anderson on Fridays' may be ambiguous in writing, but intonation will make the meaning perfectly clear in speech. Writers have to communicate such nuances in other ways. There is a limit to what can be done with the visible substance of writing; punctuation and the use of graphological conventions, such as underlining or italics, do not go very far towards duplicating the effects of intonation, stress, pausing, and change of pace. Word order can be manipulated to resolve ambiguity: 'She played tennis with Mr Anderson only on Fridays'; cleft structures are also convenient for this purpose: 'It was on Fridays that she played tennis with Mr Anderson'.

Text structuring

Readers and listeners can process text more easily if the structural relations and transitions between one part and another are made explicit. This is typically done by **discourse markers**: words and phrases whose main function is text management. English has a large number of these, for example, 'on the other hand', 'following on from that', 'a further consideration is …', 'speaking of …', 'similarly', 'nevertheless', 'on the contrary', 'mind you', 'of course', 'certainly … but', 'Right'/'OK', 'actually', 'by the way', 'anyway'. English discourse markers tend to be **register**-specific, with quite different ones being used in informal speech (for example, 'anyway') and formal writing (for example, 'whether or not that is the case'). It is not always easy to analyse the exact functions and meanings of discourse markers: some of those used in spoken English, such as 'actually' or 'I mean', are so multi-valent as to defy economical definition. Analysis is even more problematic in some other languages: German, for example, has an extensive inventory of small modal particles (for instance, *ja*, *doch*, *denn*) which express very subtle structural and attitudinal nuances.

Spoken text is often co-constructed by conversational partners, and this involves a further range of structural devices. Specific discourse markers enable English speakers, for instance, to take over the conversation ('Yes, but ...'; 'I don't know ...'), to interrupt with a shift of topic ('Speaking of ...'; 'By the way ...'), to take back the conversation ('As I was saying ...'), or to invite a response ('Right?'; 'Wouldn't you say?'). Speakers can also use 'incomplete' or 'complete' intonation contours to show whether they wish to continue speaking, or to invite their hearers to speak in their turn. Some grammatical structures exist specifically to manage the flow of conversation. English has a group of elliptical subject + auxiliary structures of this kind: question tags (for example, 'isn't it?') which ask for feedback, reply questions (for example, 'Did you really?') which act as attention signals, and short answers (for example, 'Yes, I have'). Speech also has many short formulaic 'inserts', which really form a word class of their own: 'Hi', 'Yeah', 'OK', 'Sorry', 'Look', 'Please', 'Damn!'.

Face

A central part of a speaker's context is the listener, and grammar provides ways of managing conversation so as to facilitate speaker–listener interaction and minimize threats to 'face'. Some languages, like Japanese or Thai, have a complex grammatical apparatus of **honorific** forms which enable speakers to show the appropriate degree of respect or politeness to an interlocutor. While English is more limited in this respect, it has a certain number of grammatical options for expressing respect or consideration. For instance, requests tend to be couched as questions, so as to imply that the hearer has a choice: 'Can you help me for a moment?' rather than 'Please help me'. And distancing verb forms make suggestions, requests, and questions less direct: 'I would think ...'; 'I was wondering ...'; 'How many did you want?' Intonation can be used to express consideration: a fall-rise on 'What's your name?' sounds unthreatening, while a falling **tone** might sound peremptory. Writers, too, need to express themselves in ways that show adequate respect for their readers. The English expression 'of course', for example, which credits the reader with knowledge or insights that he or she may not actually have, is a common device for mitigating the patronizing effect of giving relatively obvious or well-known information.

Formal and informal language

Probably all languages have distinct **registers** for formal and informal occasions. Both speech and writing can be more or less formal; in the nature of things, however, formal registers are more often associated with writing, and informal registers with speech. The gap between formal and informal styles perhaps partly reflects the extent to which a society is socially stratified; certainly the distance has narrowed in English with increased democratization over the last century or so. Under certain circumstances, in contrast, the registers can become completely detached. As Latin evolved in the Middle Ages, differences between formal and vernacular varieties widened to the point where the local **vernaculars** became new languages—Italian, Portuguese, Romanian, etc.—and developed their own new range of formal and informal registers.

While formality distinctions are often expressed lexically—compare English 'start'/'commence', 'tell'/'inform', 'break'/'fracture'—they may also be reflected in grammar. French, for instance, has a past tense which is virtually only used in written narrative. Formal Arabic has nominative, accusative, and dative noun **case** endings which are dropped or severely modified in informal speech. English has a certain number of grammatical structures which are felt to be intrinsically informal, and which are therefore more common in speech than in writing. Examples are contracted auxiliary phrases ('I've', 'can't'), **phrasal verbs** ('get up' as against 'rise'), and preposition stranding ('the man I bought the car from'). Some phrasal auxiliaries are most frequent in speech: 'be going to', 'have got to', 'had better'. There are also types of conditional and relative structure which, though common in spoken English, are virtually never written: 'If I'd have known, I'd have told you'; 'You do that again, you'll be in trouble'; 'I don't like songs that I don't know what they mean'; 'I want one of those cameras that you press a button and the picture comes out at the top'. Because of the traditional prestige of written norms, such structures are often condemned as incorrect, though many of them have been current in standard spoken English for centuries. This is the case for some kinds of pronoun use in coordinated subjects, like 'Me and Alice went round to Peter's last night' or 'between you and I'. Another example is the very old indefinite singular use of 'they', as in 'If anybody has lost an umbrella, could they please pick it up from the office?' With the current reduction of the prestige gap between speech and writing, some of these forms are being rehabilitated and becoming more widely regarded as acceptable.

Special kinds of text

Certain text types have their own special organizational characteristics which depart from the grammatical norms of text in general. Newspaper headlines, small ads, and similar 'reduced' genres often lack ordinary grammatical signalling devices such as articles or auxiliaries.

ARMY DOING FINE JOB, SAYS PRESIDENT

At the other extreme, literary writing may consciously play with, or flout, the normal structural conventions. Here is an example of a writer—Ernest Hemingway in *The Old Man and the Sea*— deliberately ignoring the stylistic restrictions on lexical and structural repetition that are commonly observed in English prose.

He did not remember when he had first started to talk aloud when he was by himself. He had sung when he was by himself in the old days and he had sung at night sometimes when he was alone steering on his watch in the smacks or in the turtle boats. He had probably started to talk aloud, when alone, when the boy had left. But he did not remember.

And here is Dylan Thomas in 'Poem in October' stretching English clause-structure conventions to breaking point by embedding complex prepositional phrases between verbs and their objects.

It was my thirtieth year to heaven
Woke to my hearing from harbour and neighbour wood
And the mussel pooled and the heron
Priested shore
The morning beckon
With water praying and call of seagull and rook
And the knock of sailing boats on the net webbed wall
Myself to set foot
That second
In the still sleeping town and set forth.

6

Grammar and language change

1,000 years of change in English

Beowulf, an Old English epic poem written about 1,000 years ago, starts as follows:

> *Hwæt! We Gardena   in geardagum*
> Listen! We of-spear-Danes in past-days

> *theodcyninga thrym gefrunon*
> of-tribe-kings glory have-heard

> *hu ða æthelingas ellen   fremedon.*
> how those nobles   bravery performed

> (Listen! We have heard of the glory of the kings of the fighting Danes in days of old, how those nobles performed great deeds.)

This is from the Middle English epic *Sir Gawain and the Green Knight*, written in the early fourteenth century.

> *Wrothe wynde of the welkyn wrastelez with the sunne,*
> The furious wind from the sky wrestles with the sun

> *the leuez lancen from the lynde and lygten on the grounde,*
> the leaves fly from the trees and fall on the ground

> *and al grayes the gres that grene watz ere;*
> and all grey is the grass that was green before;

> *... and thus yirnez the yere in yisterdayez mony.*
> ... and so the year passes in many yesterdays.

The Old English of *Beowulf* is clearly a foreign language, in grammar as well as vocabulary. Even the tiny extract above shows several features which differ from modern English. There are genitive and dative plural noun forms (*Gardena, theodcyninga, geardagum*) and plural verb endings (*gefrunon, fremedon*); word order is relatively free, but a subject–object–verb sentence structure is common. By contrast, the second text, written less than 350 years later (and nearly 600 years ago) is recognizably 'English'. There are still obvious differences from the modern language, but most of the complex inflectional system has disappeared, and the word order is much closer to that of today.

Mechanisms of change

All languages change over time. The process has sometimes been viewed as a type of goal-directed evolution, in which a language is progressively refined by its users to the point where it becomes an elegant and precise instrument of communication, capable of serving as a vehicle for the work of a Cicero, a Shakespeare, or a Dante. More often, perhaps, change is seen as moving in the opposite direction, with languages drifting away from their ideal state, grammatical rules being disregarded, standards dropping, and important distinctions and nuances disappearing. Both of these views take it for granted that there are 'better' and 'worse' linguistic systems, some primitive, others highly developed. In fact, however, leaving aside the special case of **pidgins** (see below, page 59), there seems to be no such thing as a primitive language, and linguists see no correlation between types of language structure and the potential for effective expression. Language change is perhaps better seen as the product of simultaneous 'downward' and 'upward' dynamics involving reorganization, reduction, and creation. On the one hand, forms of expression become routinized over time, and so lose impact and precision; on the other, language users are continually innovating in the interests of greater expressiveness. Speakers naturally pursue economy of effort, so that language forms are gradually eroded; but this is counterbalanced by hearers' need for explicitness, so that losses in one area are compensated for in another. Some changes result in greater simplification, others in greater complexity. From the point of view of communicative efficiency, the end result of these various shifts is neutral: by and large, languages continue to provide their speakers with the resources they need to achieve their purposes.

Analogy

Much language change involves analogy, with forms being modified so as to become more like other forms, as if the language wanted to tidy itself up. The verb 'like', for example, was originally used with an impersonal subject and a personal object (like modern 'please'): a sixteenth-century bible has 'The kynge had commaunded, that euery one shulde do as it lyked him'. Gradually 'like' changed so as to fit into the more widespread pattern of verbs with personal subjects, and 'me liketh this' or 'this liketh me' became 'I like this'. In a larger-scale analogical change one of several Old English pluralization patterns was generalized, so that 'shoen', for example, became 'shoes'. (The same thing still happens with foreign plurals, as in the change from 'formulae' to 'formulas'.) An example of analogical tidying in modern spoken English is the increasing use of 'would' in both clauses of a conditional sentence: 'It would be better if they would tell everybody in advance'; 'If you'd have asked me I'd have told you'. (German, French, and Spanish conditionals show similar developments.) Another modern example is an extension in the use of 'may'. Up till recently, to say that something 'may have happened' could only mean 'perhaps it happened', but 'may have …' is now increasingly used, by analogy with 'might have …', to refer to unrealized possibilities: 'That was a silly thing to do—you may have killed yourself'.

Complex systems with little functional value are particularly vulnerable to random analogical fluctuation, as if maintaining small distinctions was simply more trouble than it is worth. This can be seen in English complementation structures, where slips are common:

Ambulance services are to refuse *transporting* non-essential cases.

They have a tendency *of using* cups as ashtrays.

He was charged *of adopting* an aggressive attitude.

When such a change is repeated by other speakers, it can become institutionalized: English speakers are increasingly replacing 'for' by 'to' after the verb 'head', as in 'The ship is now heading to Liverpool'. A striking current case of breakdown in a small and functionally redundant distinction is the growing confusion between possessive and plural spellings, as in a Christmas card I received a few years ago which offered me the 'Seasons Greeting's'.

Analogy can operate between as well as within linguistic communities. Prestige varieties of a language notoriously influence other varieties. British dialects are rapidly converging on the **standard language**, while British English itself is increasingly affected by American usage. Recent grammatical changes resulting from this include the use of 'like' as a conjunction in place of 'as' ('Nobody loves you like I do'), and the extended use of 'do'-forms with 'have', as in 'Do you have a light?' instead of 'Have you got a light?'. Analogical change can cross language frontiers, with even quite dissimilar languages coming to share grammatical features, as bilingual communities modify one of their languages under the influence of the other. English in Scotland, Wales, and Ireland has grammatical **substratum** features inherited from the Celtic languages of those regions, such as the Irish **perfective** structure exemplified in 'I'm after speaking to her' ('I've spoken to her'). Romanian, Albanian, and Bulgarian, three neighbouring languages that are only distantly related, all have an inflectional definite article attached to the noun. In the multilingual village of Kupwar in India, two unrelated languages, Kannada and Urdu, have converged grammatically to the point where the local versions share numerous structures.

Phonetic erosion

Perhaps the most powerful factor in language change is phonetic erosion. Speakers naturally pronounce the ends of syllables and words with less force than the beginnings; they simplify clusters of sounds like the 'ndk' in 'handkerchief' to ease articulation; they reduce unstressed syllables like the second 'e' in 'vegetable'. Consequently sounds gradually weaken and disappear. Languages whose spelling was fixed a long time ago are haunted by phonetic ghosts, silent letters representing sounds which are no longer pronounced, as in English 'si(ghe)d', French *pe(n)s(ent)*, Irish *Dunla(oghai)re*. In the long term, this process can transform a language's grammar. When inflections are eroded, other means of expression have to be found to replace the missing elements, such as the increased use of word order or grammatical words. The differences between Anglo-Saxon and modern English are largely due to this kind of development. In English today, phonetic change is chipping away at auxiliaries in certain environments: 'We better go now'; 'I got something to tell you'; 'What you want that for?'; 'Where you going?' Another instance of erosion in modern English is the merging of 'to' with the preceding verb in some common verb + infinitive combinations: 'hafta', 'wanna', 'gotta', 'useta', 'supposeta'. If enough individual changes of this kind take place, they could ultimately lead to a restructuring of parts of the English grammatical system.

Grammaticalization

Much of grammar starts out from lexis. Where new grammatical elements are needed, either to fill developing gaps arising from phonetic erosion, or to increase the expressive power of the language, they are typically created through the **grammaticalization** of ordinary words such as nouns or verbs. This has happened, for example, with English 'have', 'do', and 'will'. If we look at their use in verb phrases like 'has seen', 'did not understand', or 'will go', we can see that their original meanings ('possess', 'act', 'want') have been completely bleached out in these contexts in favour of their grammatical functions as auxiliaries. Grammaticalization is a universal process, and there are remarkable similarities among languages all over the world in the words that are grammaticalized, the purposes for which they are used, and the routes by which they develop into auxiliaries, particles, and inflections, modifying their functions as they do so.

The words involved in grammaticalization are nearly always those with the most general meanings: 'do' rather than 'perform', 'have' rather than 'possess', 'go' rather than 'travel'. Grammaticalization typically begins in potentially ambiguous contexts, where such a word can be understood not only in its literal meaning, but also in an extended and more abstract sense. The English use of 'going to' as a future auxiliary originated in this way. If somebody said, for example, 'I am going to sell my cow', this could be interpreted not only as a description of a movement ('I am travelling to market'), but also as a statement of intention. As time went on, the 'intention' meaning became more strongly associated with the expression, and its use extended to contexts where no movement was involved, until it reached its current fully grammaticalized status.

Besides arising from verbs of movement such as 'go' or 'come', future auxiliaries are also commonly created by grammaticalizing verbs with meanings like 'be' ('I am to ...'), 'become' (German *werden*), 'wish' (English 'will', Danish *ville*, Swahili *taka*), 'be obliged to' (the original meaning of English 'shall', 'should'), and 'like' (used in the New Guinea creole language Tok Pisin). In Italian one can say that something will happen shortly by saying that it 'stands to happen': *Le porte stanno per fermarsi* is 'The doors are about to close'. Another source of future forms is the equivalent of 'have'. Latin developed a compound future made with the infinitive followed by forms of *habere* ('to have'): *cantare habeo*, meaning 'I have (something) to sing', for example, came to mean simply 'I will sing'. The forms of *habere* subsequently became reduced and turned into the inflectional endings of Latin's descendants; *cantare habeo* has become *canterò* in Italian, *je chanterai* in French.

Passive auxiliaries are often grammaticalized from words for 'be' (as in English), 'become', 'remain', 'stand', and 'come'. Past tense markers in many languages are taken from words for 'finish', such as Tok Pisin *pinis*, or the Mandarin Chinese particle *le* (from the verb *liao* meaning 'finish'); other sources are 'be' and 'do'. Words for direction can become completive markers, as in 'eat up', 'break down'. The idea of knowing how to do something can shift into more abstract senses of ability and possibility; English 'can' and German *kann* originally meant 'know'. Articles have arisen in several European languages by abstraction from demonstratives: Latin *ille* ('that') has become French *le*, Spanish *el*, etc., and English 'the' has a similar history. Both English and French negative particles are grammaticalized compound expressions; 'not' is derived from *na wiht* ('no thing'), and *ne ... pas* originally meant 'not a step'.

An interesting example of grammaticalization in modern English is the way the expression 'you guys' is effectively becoming a new **second person** plural pronoun in contrast with singular 'you', parallelling dialect forms like 'yez' and 'you all'. English is also developing two new marginal auxiliaries. The metaphorical expression 'be set to' (meaning 'be about to', like a runner in the 'set' position), is becoming common in journalistic writing in contexts like 'interest rates are set to change', where the original sense of physical action has been bleached out. And 'see', also with its literal meaning bleached out, is increasingly used to construct sentences like 'The last half year has seen a significant reduction in accident rates', providing an alternative to the 'there is' structure ('There has been … in the last year').

Grammaticalization is generally unidirectional: meanings become more abstract and generalized, and forms are commonly reduced morphologically and phonetically at the same time. Compound past tenses in European languages provide a good example of progressive meaning change. In a typical sequence, 'have' + past participle first of all takes on a resultative meaning, referring to a finished product in the present: 'I have six boxes packed'. This gradually drifts from present to past reference, while retaining a sense of present relevance: 'I have packed six boxes'—this is the current meaning of the structure in English and Spanish. In a further development, the 'present relevance' sense disappears, and the forms become used as straight past tenses, as has happened in French, Italian, and German. Formal reduction ('I have' → 'I've') accompanies the semantic development. Formal reduction is also occurring in English past modal structures ('coulda', 'woulda', 'shoulda'); and, as we have seen, it is strikingly evident in the future auxiliary 'going to'. The common informal spelling 'gonna' partly reflects the phonetic change, but in fact this extends a good deal further and is producing a set of extremely irregular merged pronoun + auxiliary forms in colloquial speech: /aŋnə/ ('I'm going to'), /jəgnə/ ('you're going to'), etc.

Speed of change

Language change does not, of course, take place overnight. Small-scale changes to specific forms can certainly spread quite quickly, especially in this age of rapid worldwide communication. The informal American use of 'was like' to mean 'said' (for example, 'She was like, "What do you mean?"') moved into the language of younger British speakers in a matter of ten years or so. But changes affecting larger linguistic systems can take centuries to work themselves out. The English progressive has been spreading through the language for several hundred years, and there are still verbs with which it is not used, although these small pockets of resistance are gradually being overrun: 'I'm understanding maths much better now'; 'She's really liking her new job'. The formation of comparatives and superlatives is following a similar path: 'more' and 'most' first took over three-syllable adjectives ('beautifullest' was possible up to the eighteenth century), and are now moving into two-syllable words: 'commoner' used to be commoner, but 'more common' is now more common. The English modal system is also changing, almost imperceptibly: **corpus** research reveals that verbs such as 'may' and 'must' are gradually becoming less frequent.

Some languages change very slowly indeed: Icelanders can read 800-year-old texts with little difficulty. At the other extreme, unusually rapid change is often due to language contact. The Dutch of the colonists in southern Africa, who were in touch with speakers of several new languages, changed much more quickly than European Dutch and underwent considerable grammatical simplification, to the point where it effectively became a different language, Afrikaans. The dramatic change in English during the 300-odd years that separate *Beowulf* from *Sir Gawain and the Green Knight* partly reflects the influence of French following the Norman Conquest. The much slower development of English over the next six or seven centuries also reflects the development of literacy, which helps to standardize languages and put a brake on development.

How did it all start?

Over very long periods, the larger processes of language change appear to be cyclical. Ordinary words are grammaticalized into auxiliaries and particles; these merge with nouns or verbs to become inflections; as phonetic erosion reduces the inflections to the point where they lose their value, new auxiliaries and particles are created to fill the gaps; these begin to merge with nouns or verbs in their turn. The initial process of grammatical creation is clearly visible in the way new languages—creoles—develop from pidgins. Pidgins are impoverished contact languages that arise to facilitate communication, usually for trade; they typically consist of vocabulary mainly drawn from the traders' language (for example, English, French, or Dutch) grafted on to a very rudimentary, often locally-based grammatical system. A pidgin is nobody's mother tongue, and pidgins lack many of the features of true languages. But in many parts of the world, such as Hawaii, New Guinea, or the Caribbean, the local pidgin has been adopted as a full-scale means of communication. Wherever this happens, the pidgin rapidly develops into a true language—a creole—with a complex and regular grammar. Creoles the world over tend to share a number of features, regardless of their diverse origins: for instance, they typically grammaticalize verbs, nouns, adjectives, or adverbs into particles or auxiliary verbs expressing time relations. While we will never know how language was born, many linguists believe that the development of creoles out of pidgins may recapitulate an original two-stage process of language evolution, whereby true language developed out of a more primitive 'protolanguage' which had little or no grammar, and would therefore have been of limited value for communication. If this was the case, grammaticalization certainly played a central part in the transformation.

7

Grammar in society: 'correctness' and standardization

Language under attack

Language change may be a natural and universal phenomenon, but people worry about it a great deal. British newspapers and journals regularly contain letters and articles complaining about falling standards, the decline of literacy, the pernicious influence of American usage, and the barbaric solecisms committed by writers and public speakers who should know better. (Such outbursts are often provoked by curiously small points of usage, such as rogue apostrophes.) Our linguistic heritage, it seems, is under threat; if we do not exercise constant vigilance, English will become impoverished and decay. Military metaphors are common; words like 'attack', 'defend', 'battle', and 'overrun' frequently occur. In some people's view, indeed, it is our very social order that is in the firing line. In a speech in 1985, Lord Tebbitt, then a prominent figure in the British government, said:

> If you allow standards to slip to the stage where good English is no better than bad English, where people turn up filthy … at school … all those things tend to cause people to have no standards at all, and once you lose standards then there's no imperative to stay out of crime.

The British are not alone. *Le Monde* regularly publishes editorials deploring what is happening to French. Many Japanese are disturbed at the way younger people speak, dropping syllables or adding redundant politeness markers in seeming defiance of the rules of grammar, and filling the language with distorted English loanwords. In a book on social change in Egypt, 'Whatever happened to the Egyptians?', Galal Amin writes:

Anyone who still remembers the respect and esteem with which Egyptians regarded the Arabic language forty or fifty years ago, cannot help but be grieved by the treatment it receives today. People used to take pride in being able to write good Arabic, in being well acquainted with the rules of Arabic grammar … All this belongs to the past.

Similar sentiments can be heard or read in any number of other countries. Somehow, it seems, people no longer know how to speak or write their own languages correctly.

What do we mean by 'incorrect'?

When someone describes another person's language as 'incorrect', he or she may be referring to any of five things:

1 Foreign learners' mistakes (for example, 'I not understand')
2 Native speakers' mistakes (for example, 'Seasons Greeting's')
3 The use of dialect forms (for example, 'I don't know nothing')
4 Alternative usage: forms used by some standard speakers and avoided by others (for example, 'different to'; 'less people')
5 The use of vernacular or slang forms (for example, 'Ann's dumped her bloke'; 'He was like, "You can't do that".').

People who are not professionally concerned with language may regard all these phenomena as instances of 'bad grammar', feeling perhaps that there is a single correct version of the language defined by rules codified in grammar books, and that deviation from these norms is rule-breaking: a sign of carelessness, ignorance, poor education, or even low intelligence. However, there are significant differences between the several types of linguistic behaviour referred to above, and not all of them can reasonably be called 'incorrect'. Most importantly, we need to distinguish *mistakes* from instances of *variation*.

Mistakes

Few people acquire new languages perfectly after late childhood, and it is normal for non-native speakers to make mistakes (including foreign language teachers, who need not feel guilty if they sometimes get things wrong). Some typical examples of mistakes made by learners of English from various language backgrounds:

'I not understand.'
'I want a dictionary who shows pronunciation.'
'Than I saw a little boy in the river that he couldn't swimming.'
'This book was writing by my uncle.'
'New car must keep in garage.'

Although these sentences are comprehensible, they are obviously incorrect—each of them conflicts with English grammatical patterns, and a native speaker, however tired or distracted, would be unlikely to produce similar utterances.

Native speakers do, however, make mistakes as well. We make slips of the tongue, talking, for example, about 'wildlife conversation' when we mean 'wildlife conservation'. We can lose our way in complicated structures, producing sentences like 'Teenage drivers are twice as likely to have accidents than the average'. This is particularly easy to do if one is forced to speak continuously without time to prepare.

'That's John McEnroe in a familiar pose, doing something to his shoelaces that never seem to be the way they want him to be.' (from a tennis commentary)

'So I think the basic point that it is necessary in order to have private capital in our industries to get the extra resources that we do want that you have to be privatized is not borne out by the facts, in other countries, and neither we should have it here also and if he's any doubts about that go and have a look at the reports that talk it.' (from a speech by John Prescott, a British politician)

Mistakes are common when speakers are off their own ground, using language that they have not quite mastered. A sign in an Oxford baker's a few years ago said 'This is a food premise. Please do not smoke.' Clearly the person who wrote it had not met the rather formal word 'premises' often enough to realize that it was only used in the plural. Formal writing notoriously presents problems of this kind. Written languages have their own grammatical characteristics which are not identical with those of speech (see Chapter 5), so that in a sense a written language is a new and unfamiliar dialect for everyone who begins to learn it.

Variation

If a dialect speaker says 'I don't know nothing' or 'I'm no working the day', or if someone says 'I will' while her neighbour says 'I shall', or if a shopper complains about 'getting ripped off', this is clearly not the same kind of thing as the mistakes referred to above. Here, the speakers are not making slips; nor are they off their own ground, trying and failing to use language they are not accustomed to handling. Whatever one might wish to say about their grammar, they are using familiar structures which they mastered as children, and which they use consistently in ways that are regular and accepted in their own communities. Utterances like these are illustrations of variation, something which is normal and natural in language. Languages vary in time (they change), in space (they have regional dialects), across society (they have class-based varieties), between individuals (speakers of the same variety do not all use it identically), and in each individual's usage (people use different styles in different situations).

Dialect forms

A language is a dialect that has an army and a navy. (Max Weinreich)

Dialect: A language variety that has everything going for it, except the government, the schools, the middle class, the law and the armed forces. (Tom McArthur)

Dialects are often regarded as corrupted forms of a language, spoken by ignorant or careless people who make mistakes because they have not learnt correct grammar, or because they cannot be troubled to get things right. In fact, however, all English dialects have a long history, going back to the distinct forms of speech of the Germanic and Scandinavian invaders who occupied Britain during the Middle Ages. And linguistic analysis shows that any well-preserved dialect has a rich and systematic grammar, even though this may be very different from that of its standard counterpart.

Interestingly, people find this easier to accept in the case of 'remote' dialects. Somebody from the south of England who says 'I wants them papers what I give you yesterday' can easily be perceived as trying and failing to produce standard grammar. On the other hand, a Scot who says 'He'll can tell us the morn' ('He'll be able to tell us tomorrow') is more readily seen as speaking an independent variety of the language with its own rule system. In fact, though, the southern speaker, just like the Scot, is using forms which are historically rooted, regular, and correct in his or her variety of the language, however much they may distress the standard English speaker next door.

The common belief that dialect forms are lazy or illogical does not stand up to examination. It is not obviously easier to say 'I didn't do nothing' than 'I didn't do anything'. On the contrary, one could argue that it takes extra effort to make pronouns and time-and-place adverbs negative so as to agree with a negative verb—French has this kind of multiple negation, and English learners of French have to work hard to get it right. And if 'I didn't do nothing' is illogical because 'two negatives make a positive' (so that it 'really' means 'I did something'), then teachers ought to be quite happy if children say 'I didn't do nothing to nobody', since logically three negatives must make a negative! In fact, of course, multiple negation is linguistically perfectly respectable, and is found in many languages. Although modern standard English does not have the structure, it existed in Old English, and survives in many dialects.

A **standard language** is not linguistically better; it is simply the variety that has been adopted for official purposes such as government and education. There is nothing intrinsically pure about 'I want' or corrupt about 'I wants' or 'I'm wanting'; 'I want' just happens to be the form used by the people whose ancestors, at one point in history, came out on top. As a result of King Alfred's victory over the Vikings in 878, the government of southern England came to be established in London, which later became the capital of the whole of Britain. Consequently, the dialect of the London area (and its later developments, profoundly influenced by Norman French), gradually evolved into the standard language—the form of English generally accepted for use in government, the law, business, education and literature. But if the Vikings, who held the north of England, had defeated

Alfred's army, the capital of modern Britain might well be York, and this book would be written in a very different kind of English.

Alternative usage

Usage varies within, as well as between, dialects. Some speakers of standard British English, for instance, say 'different to', others say 'different from'; some say 'under these circumstances', others prefer 'in these circumstances'; 'less people' and 'fewer people' are both common. 'Shall', 'if I were', 'whilst', and 'whom' are used regularly by some standard speakers, rarely or never by others. Such differences often result from language change (see Chapter 6): new forms and usages do not replace older ones overnight, and alternative ways of expressing particular meanings may coexist for some time. Indeed, some cases of divided usage remain stable for centuries: English writers were using both 'different to' and 'different from' four hundred years ago.

Individuals also have different ways of expressing themselves in different situations. Somebody might tell a friend that she 'got ripped off' in a shop; but in a complaint to the manager she might well replace the vernacular auxiliary and phrasal verb with a more formal alternative: 'I was overcharged'. We use **contractions** like 'I've' and 'don't' in informal speech and writing; in formal language full forms ('I have'; 'do not') are more usual.

As with dialect differences, these kinds of variation are a natural target for value judgements. Often, one of two variants is conventionally regarded as preferable: perhaps because it is the older form, or the form that is favoured by a traditional rule, or the one that is more common in writing or formal speech. This easily leads people who are sensitive to language to criticize other people's usage, to worry about their own, to correct their children's 'mistakes' ('*I*, not *me*! What do they teach you at school?'), and to complain about falling standards. In fact, there is generally no real basis for such judgements. A structure or expression is not incorrect because it is characteristic of casual speech rather than formal writing; the ability to deploy different styles appropriately is part of linguistic competence. And if two competing forms are widespread among speakers of a standard language (or any other variety), all that one can reasonably say is that the two forms are widespread. There is no reliable outside point of reference: no tablets of stone on which the rules of 'correct grammar' are inscribed for all eternity.

For many people, however, this is a seriously unpalatable idea, equivalent apparently to saying that 'anything goes', and that there is no way to maintain standards. Surely, (it is easy to feel) usage cannot be the only criterion for correctness—usage, after all, is exactly what is going downhill. There must be some external authority, some final court of linguistic appeal. Grammars, dictionaries, and usage guides exist in profusion: what are they for, if not to tell us the rules?

Authorities: descriptive and prescriptive rules

The word 'authority' can relate either to truth or to power. An authority on a subject is someone who can give you reliable information about it; a person in authority tells you what to do and what not to do. Accordingly, linguistic authorities produce two types of **rules**: descriptive (authoritative) and prescriptive (authoritarian).

Descriptive rules are simply accounts of linguistic *regularities*—they are, so to speak, statements of the rules that languages make for themselves. A descriptive rule might tell us that standard English adds '-s' to third person singular present verbs, that 'who' and 'whom' are both currently used as object forms, that Southern US English, somewhat like Scots, uses double modals (for example, 'I might could help you'), that Russian nouns have up to six different case endings depending on their grammatical function, or that Mandarin Chinese forms questions by adding *ma* to statements. None of these rules were consciously devised to make the languages in question work properly. They are simply the products of linguistic evolution, generated by complex mechanisms of which the speakers of the languages are quite unaware, and over which they have no conscious control.

Prescriptive rules, on the other hand, are linguistic *regulations*, rules which individuals devise in the belief that their languages need regulating, tidying up, or protecting against change. Such rules commonly appear in usage guides written for native speakers. Many were originated by eighteenth- and nineteenth-century British grammarians, often because they believed that English grammar should imitate Latin, which was considered a superior language. Some of their rules have passed into educational tradition: for example, the condemnation of **split infinitives** like 'to boldly go' (a Latin infinitive is a single word, so cannot be split), or the superstition that a preposition is a bad word to end a sentence with (Latin sentences do not end in prepositions, and anyway it was felt that a *pre*position should logically *pre*cede).

Problems with prescriptive rules

Prescriptive rules impose the beliefs of the people who devised them; they convey opinions, not facts. Neither the rule about preposition placement nor the one about split infinitives, for instance, has any basis in the reality of English grammar. (The thriller writer Raymond Chandler became so incensed at his editor's 'correction' of his split infinitives that he wrote to his publisher saying 'When I split an infinitive, God damn it, I split it so it will remain split.') An equally invalid prescriptive rule condemns singular 'they'/'them'/'their' (as in 'If somebody phones, tell them I'm out') on the spurious logical grounds that 'they' is plural. This is simply inaccurate. 'They' (like 'you') has a singular as well as a plural function: it has been used for centuries for singular indefinite reference, and an accurate account of English grammar must take note of this.

Appeals to logic are really appeals for tidiness. Sentences like 'It's me' or 'John and me saw a good film' (both typical of informal standard British English) are often condemned on the basis that a nominative (subject) form is 'logically' required in both cases. However, the choice between 'I' and 'me' is complex, depending both on syntactic environment and level of formality, and cannot be reduced to a simple, tidy rule of the kind that works for pronouns in, say, Latin, Russian, or German. Case systems actually vary considerably across languages; there is no ideal platonic conformation from which they deviate at their peril. Many languages organize themselves in ways that cut right across typical European subject–object categories, using one grammatical form both for the objects of transitive verbs and for the subjects of intransitive verbs, and a different form for the subjects of transitive verbs—rather as if we said 'He hit me, me fell down, him laughed, then me got up again and I hit him'. To argue for 'John and I saw ...' instead of 'John and me saw ...' on the 'logical' grounds that 'subjects are nominative' is rather like insisting that penguins should get up in the air because 'birds fly'.

Prescriptive condemnations often appeal to history. Since, for example, 'different' is derived from Latin *differre*, literally 'to carry away'; it is claimed that the correct preposition should be 'from', not 'to'. Unfortunately history is no better a guide to correct usage than logic. This kind of argument would have us changing most of our grammar and vocabulary, asking questions without 'do', putting verbs at the ends of clauses, and using 'lady' in its original sense of 'breadmaker' (*hlæfdige*). The best way to understand how a language works is surely to look at how it works, not at how it used to work.

Prescriptive rules also reflect the traditional feeling that the written language is more polished, elegant, and correct than the spoken vernacular, which may be regarded as low, inferior, or even incorrect by comparison. Many prescriptive grammarians consequently reject usages which are perfectly appropriate in informal speech, though they may well be out of place in more formal discourse. This is partly what motivates the condemnation of, for instance, 'John and me saw ...' or 'the people I was talking to'. A good descriptive rule would simply explain that both forms exist, while pointing out the stylistic constraints on their use.

Prescriptive rules develop their own inertia. People who worked hard to learn them when younger are reluctant to devalue their investment (and the knowledge that gives them status) by admitting that the rules are mistaken or unimportant. And, as Steven Pinker points out in *The Language Instinct*, since many prescriptive rules are so psychologically unnatural that only those with access to the right education can manage to observe them, they serve as shibboleths, differentiating the elite from the uneducated masses. ('I'm better than you because I know where to put apostrophes.')

Ripples on the ocean

People who feel that they speak their own language correctly because they 'did grammar' at school would be startled if they looked at a large reference grammar and realized how little of the mechanism of a language is actually covered in a school syllabus. During an ordinary conversation, an English speaker quickly and effortlessly makes enormous numbers of intricate grammatical manipulations and choices, operating complex rules of whose existence he or she is quite unaware, and which have little to do with the 'grammar' that the speaker learnt at school. This will have dealt, at best, with punctuation, the identification of a few grammatical categories, some stylistic questions, and the discussion of odd points of disputed usage. Such matters amount to little more than ripples on the vast ocean of the structure of English.

The feeling that languages can be defended against decline by grammatical prescription is therefore quite unrealistic. Languages develop in their own way, in accordance with complex and poorly-understood mechanisms, and there is little their speakers can do to affect the process. Prescriptive rules may change usage in small ways—if you convince enough people that 'me' is wrong in conjoined subjects, then everybody may stop using the structure, at which point it really will be incorrect. But such pronouncements have hardly any real impact on the overall development of a language.

Nor, generally, do languages (unless they are dying for lack of speakers) need such protection. Unlike, for instance, political systems or economies, languages do not naturally change for the worse. A country can see its currency devalued, experience galloping inflation, and end up by suspending payments to its creditors and appealing to the International Monetary Fund. But we do not read in the newspapers that Polish, for instance, has lost all its verbs, that Swahili is in syntactic meltdown, or that Vietnamese is in such a bad state that its speakers are reduced to communicating by waving their arms and drawing pictures. The complaint that 'the language is going to the dogs' has been heard since time immemorial. But no language with an adequate number of speakers ever seems to have arrived there.

It needs to be said, however, that the question of 'an adequate number of speakers' is gaining in relevance. As the economic and social functions of minor languages are increasingly taken over by more powerful languages such as English, there is a real danger that the number of speakers of such languages may diminish, to the point where genuine decline and ultimately language death take place. In such cases, of course, people's fears about the threat to their languages are unfortunately well founded.

The desire for standardization

If opposition to language variation and change is frequently ill-informed and unrealistic, why is it so prevalent? Partly, perhaps, for the obvious reason: that older and more influential people like to perpetuate their own standards and preferences, and to stop things slipping out of their control into the hands of another group or generation. 'Incorrect' language, like new hair-styles or fashions in music, can symbolize a worrying refusal to conform and—in some people's minds—the rejection of established authority.

This is scarcely the whole story, however. Prescriptive attitudes reflect people's instinctive desire for linguistic standardization, and this is clearly beneficial. A society will work more efficiently if all of its members understand one another easily, and the establishment of a standard language may be essential if this is to happen. A standard language also has considerable symbolic importance for a society: it constitutes a powerful statement of unity, shared values, and group identity. Standardization, especially the creation of a widely-used written standard, also slows down language change. In the short term, this reduces the extent to which different generations feel that they 'don't speak the same language'. In the long term, slower change means that a community's cultural heritage remains more accessible, since texts written centuries ago can still be read without too much difficulty.

The price of standardization

Unfortunately, standardization can exact a high price. The standard is usually the only variety that is written, so that non-standard speakers must learn a new dialect in order to achieve literacy and operate effectively in society. School systems may erect further barriers, putting such a premium on linguistic correctness that higher education and many career paths are effectively closed to those who fail to become bidialectal or to master the grammatical conventions of the written language, whatever their strengths in other areas. In this context, grammatical correctness can have powerful symbolic value: getting your language right shows the gatekeepers of society that you are good at obeying rules and respecting authority.

Language education in Britain and other countries has benefited in recent years from a more realistic understanding of the way languages work. But variation is still widely condemned as wrong. Unfortunately, it seems, the establishment of a standard language almost inevitably entails the devaluation of other varieties, often together with their speakers, who may be dismissed as 'ignorant', 'uneducated', or even 'stupid'. Such attitudes can do serious damage. Children's mother tongues are intimately bound up with their sense of personal and social identity. And the linguistic competence of even a five-year-old, whatever his or her dialect, constitutes an astounding intellectual achievement, involving the automatic and unconscious command of a range of linguistic systems and subsystems that are so complex and subtly organized that grammarians are still far from having a complete understanding of how they work. It is a great pity if, on entering the educational system and coming into contact with wider society, children are brought to believe that they have failed to learn their languages properly, and that the parents who taught them are inferior human beings who do not know how to speak correctly.

8
Grammar in the head

Investigating language

Imagine that you are trying, purely by observation, to discover how chess is played. You can watch players in action, and you can analyse recorded games, but nobody is allowed to give you information, and you have no access to a copy of the rules. Despite these handicaps, you will certainly find out some things quite quickly: for example, bishops move on diagonals, and kings move one square at a time. Other rules, however, will prove more elusive. There is a move called 'castling', involving transposing a king and a castle, which players can only perform once in a game, and which is subject to complex constraints. You would have to watch very many games, and test various hypotheses, before you could be sure of the castling rules.

Now imagine that you are investigating a type of chess which has thousands of rules and hundreds of thousands of pieces. Not all players follow exactly the same rules, and players quite often make mistakes: these mistakes are not generally marked as such in the recorded games that you study. Your situation is rather like that of a linguist trying to establish the rules of a language. The capacity for linguistic behaviour—**competence**—is shared in slightly different forms among the brains of those who engage in it; the primary evidence for the capacity—**performance**—is extraordinarily varied and complex; and the relationship between performance and competence is by no means straightforward.

From outside to inside

From the 1950s onward, the main focus of linguistic enquiry shifted from performance to competence: from grammar on the page or in the tape recording to grammar in the head. Since the publication in 1957 of Noam Chomsky's ground-breaking book *Syntactic Structures*, the purpose of grammatical investigation, for many scholars, has accordingly come to be seen as explanatory rather than descriptive. The researcher's aim, in this view, is not simply to display the regularities that can be observed to operate in examples of language production. It is also to uncover the underlying mental rules which account for, or 'generate', all of the indefinitely large range of possible grammatical sentences, and none of the ungrammatical sentences, of a language. And going beyond this, the researcher wishes ultimately to account for the characteristics of human language in general.

The idea that rules generate none of the ungrammatical sentences is crucial. While descriptive grammarians have traditionally concentrated, so to speak, on what is there, it is equally important to pay attention to what is not there—to study ways in which language users unconsciously constrain their generalizations. To take an example from English: an adequate account of reflexive pronoun use needs to explain not only why a reflexive is used in the first three of the following sentences, but why one is not used in the fourth:

1 She criticizes herself a lot.
2 He bought himself a bike.
3 I looked at myself in the mirror.
4 *When they left they took the dog with themselves.

Such questions can be explored, for example, by **elicitation tests**, which require people to produce grammatical sentences illustrating a certain pattern, or by **grammaticality judgement tests**, which ask them to rate sentences on a scale of grammaticality. Although there are problems of validity and reliability, these strategies enable researchers, up to a point, to investigate and compare infrequent structures, and thus to uncover subtle regularities and **constraints** which would not become apparent from simply examining texts. An example is the grammar of '**wh**'-extraction in English. In some cases, one can begin a question with 'what' in the main clause, even though the question relates to an element in a deeply embedded clause—for instance, 'What did John think Ann told Peter she had bought?' In other cases, this is impossible; one cannot enquire what Ann bought by saying 'What did John get cross because Ann told Peter she had bought?' By eliciting grammaticality judgements over a range of such related structures, researchers can begin to establish the underlying **generative rules** that govern and constrain native speakers' usage.

The search for powerful and economical generative rules has inevitably led grammar away from surface descriptions to more abstract formulations. A common generative-grammar account of English sentences, for example, presents noun phrases, adjective phrases, prepositional phrases and clauses as all having the same underlying abstract structure (aspects of which may not all appear in the surface forms), and thus as being generated at a 'deep' level by a single rule. The surface differences between the various structures are accounted for by further rules which relate the abstract structure to its particular spoken or written realizations. This can lead to elaborate analyses of apparently simple sentences (see Figure 8.1).

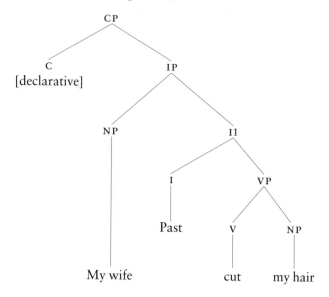

(c = complement; I = inflection)

Figure 8.1

Learnability and universal grammar

Such accounts portray language as operating according to extremely complex structural principles which are still imperfectly understood. This raises a challenging question: how is it that children manage routinely succeed in learning their mother tongues? The **input** is patchy and defective: parental speech does not seem to provide a very satisfactory, neat and tidy model from which children could easily derive the underlying rules. In some cases the input provides very little evidence indeed for the subtle and complex grammatical constraints which operate. The structures involving 'wh'-extraction referred to above, for example, are very unusual, so that children can hardly ever try them out, or be corrected for getting them wrong.

Because of this apparent **poverty of the stimulus**—the fact that linguistic knowledge seems underdetermined by the input available for learning—many linguists have claimed in recent years that some knowledge of language must be 'wired in'. We must, the argument goes, be born with a theory of language. This hypothesized genetic endowment provides children with prior information about how languages are organized, so that, once exposed to linguistic input, they can immediately start fitting the details of their particular mother tongue into a ready-made framework, rather than cracking the code from scratch without guidance.

Much of the linguistic enquiry since the 1950s has been devoted to exploring the possible characteristics of this **universal grammar** (UG), and various theoretical models have been proposed. A very influential framework is that of **principles** and **parameters**, first propounded by Chomsky in the 1980s. Briefly, the claim is that our genetic endowment includes a knowledge of the 'principles' to which all human languages conform, together with a knowledge of specific 'parameters' with respect to which they can vary.

A frequently-cited example of a principle is **structure-dependency**: the fact (discussed in Chapter 2) that linguistic operations relate to structures rather than words. For instance, if one was programming a computer to make English sentences interrogative, one could not simply instruct it to move or process the first verb. This would work for:

That man is Greek. → Is that man Greek?

But not for:

> The man who is laughing is Greek → *Is the man who laughing is Greek?

To make a successful question in the second case, a speaker or computer must be sensitive to structure, and know that the first 'is' is part of the subject noun phrase, not the main verb.

An example of a parameter is **pro-drop**. Some languages can drop subject pronouns: for instance, the normal Italian equivalent of 'he has paid' is *ha pagato* ('has paid'), and the subject pronoun is only added (*lui ha pagato*) if there is some special need to express it. Other languages are non-pro-drop: the French for 'he has paid' is *il a payé*, and without the pronoun *il* the sentence is ungrammatical. According to the theory, the Italian or French child, equipped with advance knowledge of this parameter, does not have to analyse the input at great length; a few relevant triggering examples are enough to indicate whether the language is pro-drop or non-pro-drop, and the child can set the parameter accordingly. The grammatical differences between languages, on this view, can be largely reduced to differences in the settings of a number of binary parameters.

Problems with the innatist view

The arguments for innate knowledge of language are persuasive, and the extensive research that has been devoted to the topic has added a great deal to our understanding of the grammar of various languages. None the less, UG remains extremely controversial. Any grammar which is abstract enough to describe the hypothesized common core of all the world's languages, and which contains procedures that will adequately generate from this the very different surface features of all these languages, seems doomed to be massively complex. This inevitably raises the question: how plausible is it that such a grammar could have become part of our genetic endowment? Since the 1950s, generative grammar has gone through numerous transformations, as grammarians have sought to reduce the complexity of their models while doing justice to the linguistic facts. Despite recent radical changes and the development of Chomsky's Minimalist Programme, it is not clear that the enterprise has succeeded.

Another problem relates to the learnability argument for UG—that grammar is unlearnable from the available input. Children come to know not only the hypothetically universal **core grammar** of their languages, but also a great deal of **peripheral grammar**, which is so specific to one or other language that it could not possibly be part of a genetic endowment. Like core grammar, much peripheral grammar is extremely complex—for instance, English article use or Russian inflectional morphology. This grammar, however, is necessarily learnt in some way from the input; there is no other source. This being so, one can ask why the core grammar should not also be learnable from the input in the same way (even if, in the present state of our knowledge, we cannot see exactly how this happens)?

Whether or not we have detailed 'wired-in' information about language, however, it certainly seems indisputable that human beings are equipped with a powerful predisposition to learn and/or develop language, since all normal children, regardless of differences in intelligence or environmental factors, succeed in achieving this remarkable feat.

Usage-based associative learning

The recent development of electronic corpora has transformed our ability to analyse language performance, and has consequently encouraged a move back towards descriptive investigation. This has been accompanied by a renewed focus on the role of input in language acquisition. An influential current view suggests that knowledge of language, rather than being innate, results from **usage-based associative learning**. Evidence is growing that children are capable of detecting and storing vast amounts of statistical information about regularities in linguistic input. After the earliest stages, in which they acquire unrelated **chunks** of language, and small-scale structures into which a few words can be slotted, language development proceeds (it is argued) as the bit-by-bit learning of many thousands of examples of different structures, the abstraction of regularities within them, and the unconscious tabulation of the frequency of occurrence of their components, combinations, and form-function mappings. Children, then, acquire the rules of their language by gradually seeing the dominant patterns in the input they have internalised. In the words of the cognitive psychologist Nick Ellis, 'Linguistic regularities emerge as central tendencies in the conspiracy of the database of memories of utterances.' This frequency-based account of learning claims to explain, without invoking innate knowledge, how language learners discover both regularities and constraints: how they learn not only what happens in a language, but what does not happen. The model addresses not only acquisition, but also language use: production and comprehension exploit the speaker's and hearer's detailed knowledge of the probabilities of occurrence of linguistic items and structures.

Unlike most grammatical theories, which are agnostic as regards ways in which the proposed structures and procedures might be instantiated in the brain, associative learning models are accompanied by hypotheses concerning the possible operation of **neural networks**. Research using such 'connectionist' models in computer simulations has successfully demonstrated the acquisition of some grammatical regularities from unstructured input.

Modularity: grammar in the brain

There has been considerable debate about the question of **modularity**: whether the human mind has a special module, or modules, for handling language, distinct from the faculties involved in other aspects of cognition. There seems to be good evidence that language learning, storage, and use are at least partly independent of other cognitive functions. For example, there is a **critical period** specifically for language acquisition: after a certain age, it does not seem possible for most people to achieve native-like command of a new language. And in some recorded cases where young children have been deprived of linguistic input and only started learning their language when older, their output has remained defective and ungrammatical. Further evidence for modularity comes from brain-damaged patients. Strokes or accidents sometimes cause people to lose some or all of their ability to use language, while leaving their other mental faculties apparently unimpaired. Conversely, it is possible for people with severe mental handicap to exhibit normal linguistic competence.

Until recently, language activity in the brain could only be investigated indirectly, by studying cases of brain damage. As a result of these studies it has long been known that certain areas of the brain are implicated in specific aspects of language. Damage to **Broca's area**, in front of and just above the left ear, usually results in very non-fluent speech consisting largely of nouns with few verbs, and with virtually no grammatical structure; comprehension is unimpeded. Damage to **Wernicke's area**, which is located around and under the left ear, on the other hand, results in speech which remains fluent and grammatical but which is very vague, with few precise content words; sufferers have very poor comprehension.

With modern brain-imaging techniques, it is becoming possible to monitor changes in blood flow and electrical activity during language use, and thus to gain more detailed insights into associations between brain areas and language activity. It has been shown, for example, that grammar and vocabulary use involve different patterns of excitation. However, the data that is being collected is complex and difficult to analyse, and while knowledge is growing, much more work will be necessary before a clear picture emerges. For the moment, we still know very little about how language is stored and processed. It is not clear to what extent linguistic traces are chemical or electrical; and we do not know whether our mental and linguistic representations of concepts and linguistic regularities have their physical counterparts in clusters of neurons, or in some other form. Current research suggests that much of our knowledge may be held in the form of distributed patterns of neural activation, rather than as any kind of localized representation. No doubt time will tell.

SECTION 2
Readings

Chapter 1
What is grammar?

Text 1

DEREK BICKERTON: *Language and Species*. University of
Chicago Press 1990, pages 122, 126, 128

*The thought experiment in Chapter 1 implies that language may
have evolved in two steps, with a hypothesized grammar-free
'protolanguage' leading on to full human language. Versions of
this scenario are common among writers on language evolution.
Here, Bickerton argues that present-day analogues of protolanguage contain clues to the origins of language.*

The evidence just surveyed gives grounds for supposing that there
is a mode of linguistic expression that is quite separate from
normal human language and is shared by four classes of speakers:
trained apes, children under two, adults who have been deprived
of language in their early years, and speakers of pidgin. Since this
mode emerged spontaneously in the three human classes; since
the second class includes all members of our species in their
earliest years; and since the fourth class potentially includes any
person at any time, we may regard the mode as a species characteristic. It is a species characteristic just as much as language is,
although, unlike language, it may be within the reach of other
species given appropriate training. ...

As we have seen, [grammatical items] need not be entirely absent
from protolanguage, although they are very seldom found in the
speech of children under two and will be present in ape utterances

only if the apes are explicitly taught to use them—perhaps not even then. However, even where grammatical items are found in protolanguage, their incidence will be quite low as compared with language, and their distribution will be skewed in a particular way.

Protolanguage will seldom if ever have any kind of inflection— any -*ing*s, -'ss, -*ed*s, any number- or person-agreement, and so on. It will seldom if ever have any auxiliary verbs whose function is to express tense, aspect, equation or class membership, although it may have expressions for possibility or obligation. It will lack complementizers, markers of the finite/nonfinite distinction, and conjunctions, and it will show few prepositions, articles, or demonstrative adjectives, although it may have negators, question-words, and quantifiers. In other words, the stronger the meaning element in a grammatical item, the more likely it is to appear in protolanguage. Conversely, the stronger its structural role, the less likely it is to appear. ...

If there indeed exists a more primitive variety of language alongside fully developed human language, then the task of accounting for the origins of language is made much easier.

▷ *Why should the existence of a more primitive protolanguage make 'the task of accounting for the origins of language ... much easier'?*

▷ *'... the stronger the meaning element in a grammatical item, the more likely it is to appear in protolanguage.' Why?*

Chapter 2
From simplicity to complexity: word classes and structures

Text 2
DAVID CRYSTAL: 'Gradience' in *The Cambridge Encyclopedia of Language* (2nd edn.). Cambridge University Press 1997, page 92

Crystal shows how the 'fuzziness' of word classes can be handled in a grammatical description.

Word classes should be coherent. But if we do not want to set up hundreds of classes, we have to let some irregular forms into each one. For example, for many speakers 'house' is the only English noun ending in /s/, where the /s/ becomes /z/ when the plural ending is added ('houses'). Although in theory it is 'in a class of its own', in practice it is grouped with other nouns, with which it has a great deal in common.

Because of the irregularities in a language, word classes are thus not as neatly homogeneous as the theory implies. Each class has a core of words that behave identically, from a grammatical point of view. But at the 'edges' of a class are the more irregular words, some of which may behave like words from other classes. Some adjectives have a function similar to nouns (e.g. 'the rich'); some nouns behave similarly to adjectives (e.g. 'railway' is used adjectivally before 'station').

The movement from a central core of stable grammatical behaviour to a more irregular periphery has been called 'gradience'. Adjectives display this phenomenon very clearly. Five main criteria are usually used to identify the central class of English adjectives:

(A) they occur after forms of 'to be', e.g. 'he's sad';
(B) they occur after articles and before nouns, e.g. 'the big car';
(C) they occur after 'very', e.g. 'very nice';
(D) they occur in the comparative or superlative form, e.g. 'sadder'/'saddest', 'more/most impressive'; and
(E) they occur before '-ly' to form adverbs, e.g. 'quickly'.

We can now use these criteria to test how much like an adjective a word is. In the matrix below, candidate words are listed on the left, and the five criteria are along the top. If a word meets a criterion, it is given a +; 'sad', for example, is clearly an adjective ('he's sad', 'the sad girl', 'very sad', 'sadder'/'saddest', 'sadly'). If a word fails the criterion, it is given a – (as in the case of 'want', which is nothing like an adjective: *'he's want', *'the want girl', *'very want', *'wanter'/'wantest', *'wantly').

	A	B	C	D	E
happy	+	+	+	+	+
old	+	+	+	+	–
top	+	+	+	–	–
two	+	+	–	–	–
asleep	+	–	–	–	–
want	–	–	–	–	–

The pattern in the diagram is of course wholly artificial because it depends on the way in which the criteria are placed in sequence; but it does help to show the gradual nature of the changes as one moves away from the central class, represented by 'happy'. Some adjectives, it seems, are more adjective-like than others.

▷ *How do* my, red, other, glass, lost *and* mere *fit into the matrix?* *Try to fit other words into the matrix.*

▷ *Do you think it is possible to make a similar matrix for nouns?* *Try to make one that will show 'gradience' for these words:* book, furniture, means, police, rich, fun, writing, James, expect.

▷ *Do you think it would be valuable for (a) primary-school children or (b) secondary-school children to learn about gradience in the grammar of their own language?*

Texts 3 and 4

BERTRAND RUSSELL: *History of Western Philosophy* (first published 1946). Routledge 2004, page 540
BERTRAND RUSSELL: *Introduction to Mathematical Philosophy*. Allen and Unwin 1919, Chapter 16, page 172

Some philosophers have argued that, because ordinary languages are vague and ambiguous, valid argument is only possible in artificial languages in which all terms have precise definitions. In these two short texts, Russell outlines the views of Leibniz (1646–1716), and offers his own opinion of ordinary language.

Text 3

[Leibniz] cherished throughout his life the hope of discovering a kind of generalized mathematics, which he called *Characteristica Universalis*, by means of which thinking could be replaced by calculation. 'If we had it,' he says, 'we should be able to reason in metaphysics and morals in much the same way as in geometry and analysis [a branch of mathematics]. If controversies were to arise, there would be no more need of disputation between two philosophers than between two accountants. For it would suffice to take their pencils in their hands, to sit down to their slates, and to say to each other (with a friend as witness, if they liked): 'Let us calculate.'

Text 4

The proposition 'Socrates is a man' is no doubt equivalent to 'Socrates is human,' but it is not the very same proposition. The 'is' of 'Socrates is human' expresses the relation of subject and predicate; the 'is' of 'Socrates is a man' expresses identity. It is a disgrace to the human race that it has chosen to employ the same word 'is' for these two entirely different ideas—a disgrace which a symbolic logical language of course remedies.

▷ *Do you agree that the vagueness of ordinary language is a 'disgrace to the human race'; or are there good reasons for this vagueness?*

▷ *Do you think it is possible to eliminate or reduce misunderstandings by devising more precise means of communication than ordinary language?*

▷ *Do you agree that 'is' has different functions in 'Socrates is a man' and 'Socrates is human'?*

▷ *Do you know a language which has different equivalents of English 'is', depending on the exact meaning?*

Text 5

KEITH BROWN and JIM MILLER (eds.): *Concise Encyclopedia of Syntactic Theories.* Pergamon 1996, pages xiv–xv

This text looks at the nature of grammars, and deals with an issue discussed briefly at the end of Chapter 2: the ways in which grammatical models vary in their focus and choice of fundamental units.

Traditionally grammars of languages describe the structure of words, phrases, clauses, and sentences, employing concepts relating to morphology (e.g., stem, root, affix) and syntax (e.g., phrase, head, modifier, construction, word order). ... Experienced users of a language probably consult dictionaries more than grammars. They have come to terms with the tense, aspect, mood, case, and transitivity systems of the language and can use word order, highlighting devices, and sentence connectives to construct longer texts out of sentences.

... Formal grammars are constructed to handle the various types of information mentioned above, although as yet no grammar handles all the types. Some grammars are designed to generate (give exact specifications of) syntactic constructions, especially the arrangements and dependency relations of constituents. With a given construction some grammars associate a semantic structure, expressed in logical formalism, and a phonological/phonetic structure. With respect to syntax, some grammars specify the structure of words, phrases, and clauses while others focus on words and treat phrases as secondary items. Most grammars recognize syntactic constructions. At the limits, Government and Binding and Principles and Parameters [two approaches to generative grammar: see Chapter 8] see individual constructions as secondary and give primacy to general constraints each applying to a range of different constructions .... Construction Grammar ... takes constructions as central and fundamental. Some models of grammar neglect basic syntactic structure, attending instead to the functions of different constructions in text. These models concentrate on the linguistic representation of situations focusing on questions such as: Does a given situation involve an action or a state? What roles are there? Is the agent expressed or not? If it is, is it expressed by a central clause constituent such as a subject noun phrase or by a peripheral constituent such as a prepositional phrase? Is the patient expressed or not? Do the answers to these questions affect the shape of the verb in a given clause?

▷ *Linguists have a vast amount of highly visible language data to examine; and yet they disagree massively about what they are looking at—about the grammatical organization of languages, and of language in general. This seems strange. What might the reasons be?*

Chapter 3
Grammar in the world's languages

Text 6
JOHN MCWHORTER: *The Power of Babel: A Natural History of Language*. Heinemann 2001, pages 188–9

Chapter 3 looks at different ways in which languages (a) exploit the formal resources of grammar and (b) express meanings through grammar. This text comprises a part of McWhorter's description of an extreme case of formal complexity.

For my money, there are few better examples than Fula of West Africa of how astoundingly baroque, arbitrary, and utterly useless to communication a language's grammar can become over the millennia and yet still be passed on intact to innocent children. Fula has as many as sixteen 'genders' in the sense that we parse the concept in Indo-European languages, and which gender a noun belongs to is only roughly predictable beyond the one gender that contains humans. Moreover, within each gender, the marker varies arbitrarily according to the noun: *leemuu-re* 'orange' but in the same gender class is *loo-nde* 'jar'. Adjectives, instead of taking a 'copy' of the marker variant its noun takes, take their own particular marker variant, which must be learned with the adjective. Thus a big orange is not *leemuu-re mau-re*, but *leemuu-re mau-nde*.

Fula is even more elaborated than this. There are often not just two, or even three, but four variants of the gender marker. Thus in our 'gender' that contains oranges and jars, the marker turns up as *-re* in *leemuu-re* 'orange', as *-nde* in *loo-nde* 'jar', but as *-de* in *tummu-de* 'calabash'; in another gender, a strip is *lepp-ol*, a feather is *lilli-wol*, a belt is *taador-gol*, whereas a leather armlet is *boor-ngol*. Besides this, like any language, Fula has its irregulars: in one gender, you have to know not only that a noun will take either *-u*, *-wu*, *-gu* or *-ngu* as its marker, but also that the occasional noun will go its own way and take *-ku* instead.

… [F]or most Fula nouns, when we tack a new diminutive or augmentative gender marker onto the *end* of the word, simultaneously the consonant at the *beginning* of the word changes in some way—and as often as not there are two different consonants that it might become, depending on which of the genders we are switching to. *A man* is *gor-ko*. The article for the augmentative 'gender' is *-ga* (this is actually one of four variants for this gender plus an additional one that pops up irregularly!), but one says not *gor-ga* but *ngor-ga*. There is another consonant change to make *gor* plural: the plural article … is *-be*, but one says not *gor-be* but *wor-be*.

▷ *Can you think of examples in other languages of formal complexity that seems to have little or no functional value?*

▷ *What do you think are the most formally difficult things in your own language for foreigners to learn correctly?*

Text 7

EDWARD SAPIR: *Language*. Harcourt, Brace. 1921, pages 92-3

In this extract from Sapir's classic book, he talks about how different cultures encode different aspects of reality in the grammars of their languages.

In the Chinese sentence 'Măn kill duck', which may be looked upon as the practical equivalent of 'The man kills the duck', there is by no means present for the Chinese consciousness that childish, halting, empty feeling which we experience in the literal English translation. The three concrete concepts—two objects and an action—are each directly expressed by a monosyllabic word which is at the same time a radical element; the two relational concepts—'subject' and 'object'—are expressed solely by the position of the concrete words before and after the word of action. And that is all. Definiteness or indefiniteness of reference, number, personality as an inherent aspect of the verb, tense, not to speak of gender—all these are given no expression in the Chinese sentence, which, for all that, is a perfectly adequate communication—provided, of course, there is that context, that background of mutual understanding that is essential to the complete intelligibility of all speech. Nor does this qualification impair our argument, for in the English sentence too we leave unexpressed a large number of ideas which are either taken for granted or which have been developed or are about to be developed in the course of the conversation. Nothing has been said, for example, in the English ... sentence as to the place relations of the farmer, the duck, the speaker, and the listener. Are the farmer and the duck both visible or is one or the other invisible from the point of view of the speaker, and are both placed within the horizon of the speaker, the listener, or of some indefinite point of reference 'off yonder'? In other words, to paraphrase awkwardly certain latently 'demonstrative' ideas, does this farmer (invisible to us but standing behind a door not far away from me, you being seated yonder well out of reach) kill that duckling (which belongs to you)? or does that farmer (who lives in your neighbourhood and whom we see over there) kill that duckling (that belongs to him)? This type of demonstrative elaboration is foreign to our way of thinking, but it would seem very natural, indeed unavoidable, to a Kwakiutl Indian.

▷ *Do you think there are advantages in having time, number, or definiteness expressed grammatically?*

▷ *What might be the advantages to Kwakiutl Indians of having the spatial and possessive relations which Sapir mentions incorporated in their grammar?*

▷ *If you know two languages well, try to think of meanings which are expressed in the grammar of one but not the other.*

Text 8
DEDRE GENTNER and SUSAN GOLDIN-MEADOW: 'Whither Whorf' in *Language in Mind*. MIT Press 2003, page 4

The Sapir-Whorf hypothesis, after some decades of neglect, is receiving renewed attention from researchers. In this text, the authors explain why the claim (which they call the 'Whorfian hypothesis') seems reasonable.

Why would anyone ever come up with the hypothesis that the language we speak shapes the thoughts we think? Consider a plausible scenario. When retelling an event, speakers of Turkish are required by their language to indicate whether they themselves actually witnessed that event … . Of course, the speaker knows whether she witnessed the event. However, she may not be interested in conveying this bit of information to the listener. Speakers of English have the option (which they often exercise) of leaving out whether they actually witnessed the event they are retelling—speakers of Turkish do not. After many years of routinely marking whether they witnessed an event, it is possible that Turkish speakers will tend to encode whether an event has been witnessed, whether or not they are talking. That is, Turkish speakers may habitually attend to this feature of the world much more than English speakers do. In other words, their way of viewing the world may have been altered just by becoming speakers of Turkish as opposed to English. This is the kind of reasoning that underlies the Whorfian hypothesis.

▷ *Do you find the authors' scenario plausible?*

Chapter 4
Grammar and vocabulary

Text 9

ALISON WRAY: 'How far can you go? Modelling the relationship between grammar and lexis'. Unpublished summary of a talk given at St Mary's College, Twickenham, 18 June 2004, based on ideas in A. Wray 2002. *Formulaic Language and the Lexicon.* Cambridge University Press

Wray proposes a model of the 'mental lexicon' which differs interestingly from that found in more traditional theories. She suggests that this model may help to account for the difficulty adults have in learning foreign languages.

The study of language as a whole, and language teaching in particular, is challenged by the perpetual question of where vocabulary ends and grammar starts. Answering this question could help explain why L2 learners struggle so hard to sound nativelike (idiomatic). The problem may lie in a long-held assumption that the mental lexicon is 'atomic'—does not store anything that could be broken down further. The atomic lexicon model makes three interesting predictions:

a) All regular formulations of a message are equally nativelike ways of expressing that message
b) Irregularity is awkward and undesirable
c) Acquiring a fully regular language will be easier than acquiring a normal (natural) language.

However, research reveals that none of these predictions is true. There is more to sounding nativelike than just knowing the words and rules of a language: you have to know what is idiomatic, that is, the preferred formulation in a particular speech community. Irregularity pervades languages and as fast as one irregular formulation drops out of the language others enter it. And research by Benjamin K. Bergen shows that children acquiring Esperanto, a perfectly regular language, not only miss seeing its regularities, but actually introduce irregularities (*Journal of Child Language*: 'Nativization processes in L1 Esperanto', volume 28/3, pages 575–95).

Furthermore, psycholinguistic evidence has long since demonstrated that the atomic lexicon is not as atomic as it 'ought' to be, and this offers a clue to a different way of conceptualising how we store words and phrases.

I propose that the lexicon is *heteromorphic*—made up of different sized forms, including not only morphemes, words, etymological relics and idioms, but also any other, larger, strings that are useful to us: common phrases, common collocations and clauses with gaps in. Such a lexicon is less efficient in terms of storage, but storage efficiency does not seem to be crucial for the brain. Most importantly, exactly what the heteromorphic lexicon contains will depend on the input we are exposed to and what we customarily need to say.

Items become stored largely through a process of *needs only analysis*—the brain only processes material to the point where it stops displaying evidence of flexibility. (In contrast, the atomic lexicon model is based on the idea that everything is reduced to its smallest components *on principle*, as a response to an innate need to identify and use them with full creativity.)

The heteromorphic lexicon helps explain why adult learners of an L2 struggle to sound idiomatic: as a result of age and education, they treat their input differently from native speakers. They break it down into smaller components, and so do not have the larger strings ready-stored. As a result, they over-generate, producing meaningful, grammatical sentences that are simply not always nativelike. This is borne out by the results of recent experiments that I have conducted, in which adult L2 learners tried to reproduce memorised sentences without changing them —and could not.

We can conclude that the line between lexis and grammar must be drawn flexibly, and that the adult L2 learner may struggle in vain for full idiomaticity unless/until a lengthy spell of residence provides the opportunity to override the prejudices of the normal learning style.

▷ *Does your experience of learning and using foreign languages seem to bear out (a) Wray's notion of a heteromorphic lexicon, and (b) her suggestion that adult foreign-language learners are better at analysing input than at learning chunks?*

Text 10

ELIZABETH BATES and JUDITH C. GOODMAN: 'On the inseparability of grammar and the lexicon' in M. Tomasello and E. Bates (eds.): *Language Development*. Blackwell 2001, pages 134–5

The authors discuss the way in which theoretical linguistics has moved towards breaking down the barriers between grammar and vocabulary.

Linguistics is a field that is known for controversy. However, one general trend has characterized recent proposals in otherwise very diverse theoretical frameworks: more and more of the explanatory work that was previously handled by the grammar has been moved into the lexicon. In some frameworks [e.g. Chomsky's], the grammatical component that remains is an austere, 'stripped down' system characterized by a single rule for movement and a set of constraints on the application of that rule. In this theory, the richness and diversity of linguistic forms within any particular language are now captured almost entirely by the lexicon—although this is now a very complex lexicon that includes propositional structures and productive rules that govern the way elements are combined. The trend towards lexicalism … reaches its logical conclusion in a framework called Construction Grammar, in which the distinction between grammar and the lexicon has disappeared altogether. Instead, all elements of linguistic form are represented within a heterogeneous lexicon that contains bound morphemes, free-standing content and function words, and complex phrase structures without terminal elements (e.g., the passive). This lexicon can be likened to a large municipal zoo, with many different kinds of animals. To be sure, the animals vary greatly in size, shape, food preference, lifestyle, and the kind of handling they require. But they live together in one compound under common management. …

This does not mean that grammatical structures don't exist (they do), or that the representations that underlie grammatical phenomena are identical to those that underlie single-content words (they are not). Rather, we are suggesting that the hetero- geneous set of linguistic forms that occur in any natural language (i.e. words, morphemes, phrase structure types) may be acquired and processed by a unified processing system, one that obeys a common set of activation and learning principles. There is no need for discontinuous boundaries.

▷ *Is the 'heterogeneous lexicon' described here the same as Wray's 'heteromorphic lexicon' (Text 9), or are there differences? Would Wray's lexicon contain the passive?*

▷ *If grammatical regularities are reclassified as aspects of the lexicon, does this make a genuine difference to our view of language, or is it simply a terminological change?*

Text 11

MARTHA JONES and SANDRA HAYWOOD: 'Facilitating the acquisition of formulaic sequences' in N. Schmitt (ed.): *Formulaic Sequences: Acquisition, Processing and Use.* John Benjamins 2004, page 273

The authors suggest that a command of formulaic language is important for successful academic work.

Both undergraduates and postgraduates serve a kind of apprentice-ship in their chosen discipline, gradually familiarising themselves not only with the knowledge and skills of their field, but also with the language of that field, so that they become capable of expressing their ideas in the form that is expected. As they do this, their use of formulaic sequences enables them, for example, to express technical ideas economically, to signal stages in their discourse and to display the necessary level of formality. The absence of such features may result in a student's writing being judged as inadequate. Commenting on the work of a Jordanian student, one lecturer wrote 'the use of English ... is a problem throughout the essay. By this I do not mean your English is poor or unintelligible but it is too colloquial and the phraseology is poor'... . On the other hand, familiarity with and control of the language of their field indicates their membership of the group, in this case, the community of their chosen academic discipline. In addition, when the writing style is conventional, it attracts little attention. This lightens the processing load for the reader and allows the writer's message to be more easily perceived.

▷ *Is a command of all types of formulaic sequence essential for appropriate academic discourse; or are there more and less important categories?*

▷ *How far is it necessary, and realistic, to require non-native-speaker students to aim at a native-like command of formulaic sequences?*

Chapter 5
Grammar in spoken and written text

Text 12
GUNNEL TOTTIE: 'Conversational style in British and American English' in K. Aijmer and B. Altenberg (eds.): *English Corpus Linguistics: Studies in Honour of Jan Svartvik*. Longman 1991, page 255

Tottie discusses 'marginal words', and in particular 'back-channels', a type of linguistic item which has been neglected by linguists but which is important for the organization of discourse.

One largely uncharted area of conversational style has to do with the use of what Tannen refers to as 'ways of showing that you're interested', often called 'backchannels'. Backchannels are the sounds (and gestures) made in conversation by the current non-speaker, which grease the wheels of conversation but constitute no claim to take over the turn. On the basis of informal observations, it seemed to me that these were among the features of language that differ according to regional background, in this case between British and American English, but I could find no corroboration of this in the literature.

One reason why the use of backchannels has attracted little previous attention among linguists is certainly that they occur only in spoken language, long a stepchild of descriptive linguistics. Furthermore, they are mostly realised by ... 'marginal words', i.e. vocalizations that are usually rendered as *m, mhm, uh-(h)uh*, and the like in writing. These items are only rarely captured by writers of fiction or drama and are badly represented or left out by most dictionaries. As Svartvik points out, the 'lexicographer still has a tendency to consider the occurrence of a word in print the chief or sole criterion for its inclusion in the dictionary'—yet *m*, with various intonation patterns, is one of the most frequent 'words' in British English conversation; thus *m*, with falling intonation, ranked 3 1 and was one of the most common lexical items in the London-Lund corpus of Spoken English. Similarly, *m* is one of the most common items in spoken Swedish but is missing from all dictionaries of Swedish.

There is thus a vicious circle: because words of this kind have been regarded as marginal words, they have attracted little research, in spite of the fact that they are used for a large number of functions in spoken communication—as hesitation signals, feedback signals in question-answer sequences, affirmative and negative responses, etc.

▷ *This text mentions three examples of backchannels:* m, mhm *and* uh-(h)uh. *Can you think of other backchannels in English, or of equivalents in other languages you know?*

▷ *Are backchannels vocabulary or grammar?*

Text 13

MICHAEL McCARTHY: 'Units of description in grammar and discourse' in *Spoken Language and Applied Linguistics.* Cambridge University Press 1 9 9 8, pages 8 0–2

McCarthy examines the grammar of a piece of transcribed conversation, and argues that it is not well handled by the kind of analysis traditionally applied to written texts. In particular, he questions the usefulness of such notions as 'main clause' and 'subordinate clause'.

[Two students are talking about what people are going to wear to a forthcoming ball.]

<S 01> I really am I'm so pissed off that everyone's erm everyone's going to be wearing erm
<S 02> Cocktail dresses.
<S 01> I don't, I really don't see the point the whole point of a ball is that you wear like a proper dress
<S 02> Wear a ball dress I know I mean my dress is huge.

<S 01> So is Nicola definitely going to, erm is Nick definite
<S 02>   └Well   she
she says she is but if she sees everybody else wearing a cocktail
dress she's bound to fork out the money she's got loads of
money.
<S 01> Cos mum said to me you know that she would buy me like
a a little black dress but the thing is then I wouldn't feel right
you know.
<S 02> Well, I mean you wear a
<S 01>   └She, but you know she means like something from
like, erm, Miss Selfridge or something.
<S 02> Yes if, I mean you wear a little black dress just to, you know
<S 01> Clubbing or something.
<S 02> To a party
<S 01> Yeah exactly.

The first 'sentence' seems to be spoken by two speakers, with
<S 02> providing the object of <S 01>'s verb *wearing*. In the next
pair of utterances, <S 02> repeats <S 01>'s direct object in a slightly reworded form (<S 01> … *wear like a proper dress* <S 02>
Wear a ball dress). In the final utterances of the extract, both speakers 'complete' the same clause, but with different constituents
(*Clubbing or something/To a party*). How do we analyse 'other-
completed clauses/sentences'? How do we analyse 'other-repeated
grammar'? Are <S 02>'s utterances here part of <S 01>'s 'sentences',
or units of their own? Where both complete the clause, are the two
different constituents of equal status in its structure? A grammar-
in-discourse approach sees structure as a collaborative/negotiative
process rather than as a deterministic product. Within the relevant
factors of description it includes real-time contextual features such
as turn-taking, repetition and joint construction by more than one
party.

There are some items in [the conversation] which do not seem
to be main clauses:

> *that everyone's erm everyone's going to be wearing cocktail
> dresses that you wear like a proper dress*
> (she says) *she is*
> *if she sees everybody else wearing a cocktail dress*
> (mum said to me) *that she would buy me a little black dress*

The first two are complement-clauses (thus not subordinate in the true sense), which are frequent in conversational language. Two are reported clauses within speech reports (also frequent ...), which are arguably 'main clauses' transferred from other discourses. Only one seems to be a conventional conditional subordinate clause with *if*. The clause *Cos* [Because] *mum said to me you know that she would buy me like a little black dress* would seem superficially to be a candidate for subordination, but (a) it is separated from its 'main' clause by an intervening turn, and (b) it seems simply to *add* background information rather than place any restriction or contingency on the main portion. It means 'this is the reason I'm asking about Nicola' and does not exercise any causal conditioning on the main clause. It seems more reasonable, therefore, to treat the *cos* clause as non-subordinate, but discoursally as providing background/supporting information. ...

This kind of problem of classification has led some linguists to propose abandoning the notion of 'subordination' altogether when it comes to describing and explaining spoken grammar ... and to advocate substituting the clause as a more viable basic unit for spoken language than the sentence ... . Another good reason for advocating this is that some sentence-configurations, for example non-finite clauses/prepositional clauses plus main clause (such as *On leaving the building she noticed a black car*), which are found in formal written language, are extremely rare in conversation. ... Grammar becomes discourse when conventional sentence-based units of description fail to account for the facts, suggesting an alternative descriptive model based more on units of information and interpersonal considerations generated within real contexts.

▷ *What do you consider McCarthy means by 'Grammar becomes discourse'? Is he saying that 'grammar' should be abandoned as a framework for analysing conversation, or that a different kind of 'grammar' is required? Or is his position not made clear in this text?*

▷ *Do McCarthy's comments suggest that we should not teach grammar, as currently described, in courses of spoken English?*

Chapter 6
Grammar and language change

Text 14

JEAN AITCHISON: 'Petrified phrases' in *Language Change: Progress or Decay?* (3rd edn.). Cambridge University Press 2001, pages 116–18

Aitchison looks at two interesting examples of grammaticalization in English, whereby prepositional phrases have developed into discourse markers.

Grammaticalization extends like a blanket across a whole range of constructions. It encompasses not only chopped down words, but also petrified phrases, as with **discourse markers**, the words and phrases which link one section of speech or writing to another.

Take the English phrase *instead of*. In old English, *stede* meant 'place', as in *to thaem stede* 'to that place' (c. 880), a usage still found in the word *homestead*. Then *stede* was used in a phrase meaning 'in the place of', referring to one person substituting for another:

> Matthias … waes gecoren on Judan stede. (c. 1000)
> 'Matthias was chosen in Judas' place.'

This substitution was extended to abstract actions, as in Chaucer's *Canterbury Tales*:

> Therfore **in stede** of wepynge and preyeres
> Men moote yeve silver to the povre freres (c. 1388)
> 'Therefore instead of weeping and prayers, people should give silver to the poor priests.'

At a later stage, *in stede* joined up to become *instead*.

Or consider the word *indeed*. At first, *deed* was a simple noun, as it also still is in modern English:

> in thohut, in speeche and in dede (c. 1300)
> 'in thought, in speech and in deed'

Next, it came to be an adverb attached towards the front of its clause, where it highlighted an unexpected fact:

they [the teacher] sometyme purposely suffring [allowing] the more noble children to vainquysshe ... though **in dede** the inferiour chyldren have more lerning. (1531)

In the next century, it coalesced into a single word, and became a full discourse marker. As with *instead*, the movement was from manner adverb, to sentence adverb, to discourse marker.

▷ *Can you think of similar examples of the development of discourse markers in English or other languages?*

Text 15

JEAN AITCHISON: 'The reason why: sociolinguistic causes of language change' in *Language Change: Progress or Decay?* (3rd edn.). Cambridge University Press 2001, pages 133–4

In this second extract from the same book, Aitchison discusses the difficulty of accounting for language change.

For centuries, people have speculated about the causes of language change. The problem is not one of thinking up possible causes, but of deciding which to take seriously. ... As one [linguist] noted: 'Linguists are a marvellously clever bunch of scholars; there is really *no limit* to the imaginative, elegant and intellectually satisfying hypotheses they can dream up to account for observed linguistic behaviour.'

In the past, language change has been attributed to a bewildering variety of factors ranging over almost every aspect of human life, physical, social, mental and environmental. At one time, for example, there was a suggestion that consonant changes begin in mountain regions due to the intensity of expiration in high altitudes. 'The connection with geographical or climatic conditions is clear,' asserted one scholar, 'because nobody will deny that residence in the mountains, especially in the high mountains, stimulates the lungs.' Luckily this theory is easily disprovable, since Danish, spoken in the flat country of Denmark, seems to be independently undergoing a set of extensive consonant changes—unless we attribute the Danish development to the increasing number of Danes who go to Switzerland or Norway for their summer holidays each year, as one linguist ironically suggested.

Even when we have eliminated the 'lunatic fringe' theories, we are left with an enormous number of possible causes to take into consideration. Part of the problem is that there are several different causative factors at work, not only in language as a whole, but also in any one change. Like a road accident, a language change may have multiple causes. A car crash is only rarely caused by one overriding factor, such as a sudden steering failure, or the driver falling asleep. More often there is a combination of factors, all of which contribute to the overall disaster. Similarly, language change is likely to be due to a combination of factors.

▷ Aitchison gives an amusing example of a ridiculous explanation for language change. Can you invent another improbable explanation?

▷ Later in the chapter from which this text is taken, Aitchison talks about sociolinguistic causes of language change: fashion, foreign influence, and social need. Can you think of examples of change that come under one or more of these headings?

Chapter 7
Grammar in society: 'correctness' and standardization

Text 16
STEVEN PINKER: 'The language mavens' in *The Language Instinct*. Allen Lane/Penguin 1994, page 370

In a persuasive argument by analogy, Pinker attacks prescriptive attitudes to language.

Imagine that you are watching a nature documentary. The video shows the usual gorgeous footage of animals in their natural habitats. But the voiceover reports some troubling facts. Dolphins do not execute their swimming strokes properly. White-crowned sparrows carelessly debase their calls. Chickadees' nests are incorrectly constructed, pandas hold bamboo in the wrong paw, the song of the humpback whale contains several well-known errors, and monkeys' cries have been in a state of chaos and degeneration for hundreds of years. Your reaction would probably be, What on earth could it mean, for the song of the humpback whale to contain an 'error'? Isn't the song of the humpback whale whatever the humpback whale decides to sing? Who is this announcer, anyway?

But for human language, most people think that the same pronouncements not only are meaningful but are cause for alarm. Johnny can't construct a meaningful sentence. As educational standards decline and pop culture disseminates the inarticulate ravings and unintelligible patois of surfers, jocks, and valley girls, we are turning into a nation of functional illiterates: misusing *hopefully*, confusing *lie* and *lay*, treating *data* as a singular noun, letting our participles dangle. English itself will steadily decay unless we get back to basics and start to respect our language again.

To a linguist or psycholinguist, of course, language is like the song of the humpback whale. The way to determine whether a construction is 'grammatical' is to find people who speak the language and ask them.

▷ *Do you agree with Pinker's argument that 'To a linguist …language is like the song of the humpback whale'?*

▷ *In the last sentence of the text, Pinker suggests a way of determining whether a construction is 'grammatical'. Do you think this is a reliable method?*

Text 17

GUY COOK: 'Description versus prescription' in *Applied Linguistics*. Oxford University Press 2003, pages 16–18

Cook offers a more balanced view of the prescriptive/descriptive issue, suggesting that arguments against prescriptivism need to be tempered by a concern for social reality.

While all of these arguments appear to have a kind of relentless logic to them, they depend on a detachment from social reality and are very much at odds with a deeply felt public view of language. It is all very well to say that, linguistically speaking, correctness is not a valid concept, but to many people deciding what counts as correct is *the* single most important issue about their language, and for linguistics, the discipline which claims to study language, to refuse to engage with this debate is perceived as at best incomprehensible, and at worst subversive and perverse. Linguists may assume a superior air and insist that their concern is with objective descriptions, but in taking this stance they necessarily distance themselves from people's everyday experience of language.

… We might observe that, as is often the case in such disputes, it is certainly not that academic experts are necessarily right and lay opinion just wrong-headed. Academics do not have a monopoly either on knowledge or on rational argument. The same is true in many analogous domains—for example, medicine, nutrition, or childcare—where everyday activity, vital to people's well-being, is also the subject of academic research. Thus, while there is force in descriptivist arguments, there are also valid reservations to be made about them:

1 To talk about a language at all, there must be some pre-existing notion of what does and does not count as an example. Descriptivists may accept, as instances, some examples of dialectal forms which hard-line prescriptivists would exclude, but there are always others—from another language, for example—which they reject. Thus, they are drawing the boundary round a language in a different place, not abandoning the notion of boundaries altogether.

2 In deciding what does count as an example of a language, linguists often base their decisions upon native-speaker use or judgement. This, however, simply shifts the criterion away from what is said to the person who says it. It also runs the danger of becoming circular, i.e. native speakers provide valid examples of the language; valid examples of the language are provided by native speakers.

3 Despite descriptivist insistence on the equality of all varieties, it is nevertheless the standard which is most often used in their analyses while other varieties are described as departures from it.

4 If linguists are concerned with describing and explaining facts about language, then the widespread belief in prescriptivism, and the effect of this belief on language use, is itself a fact about language which needs describing and explaining.

5 Paradoxically, to advocate description and outlaw prescription is itself prescriptive.

> Are all of Cook's five 'valid reservations' equally valid, in your view? Which do you feel is/are the strongest?

> Do you feel the benefits of standardization in language, discussed in Chapter 7, outweigh the disadvantages in all social contexts, in some (which?), or in none?

Chapter 8
Grammar in the head

Text 18

NOAM CHOMSKY: *New Horizons in the Study of Language and Mind*. Cambridge University Press 2000, pages 6–7

Chomsky discusses linguistic complexity, in the light of his view that all languages are minor variations on a general pattern determined by an innate universal grammar.

The earliest attempts to carry out the program of generative grammar quickly revealed that even in the best studied languages, elementary properties had passed unrecognized, that the most comprehensive traditional grammars and dictionaries only skim the surface. The basic properties of languages are presupposed throughout, unrecognized and unexpressed. That is quite appropriate if the goal is to help people to learn a second language, to find the conventional meaning and pronunciation of words, or to have some general idea of how languages differ. But if our goal is to understand the language faculty and the states it can assume, we cannot tacitly presuppose 'the intelligence of the reader'. Rather, this is the object of inquiry.

The study of language acquisition leads to the same conclusion. A careful look at the interpretation of expressions reveals very quickly that from the earliest stages, the child knows vastly more than experience has provided. That is true even of simple words. At peak periods of language growth, a child is acquiring words at a rate of about one an hour, with extremely limited exposure under highly ambiguous conditions. The words are understood in delicate and intricate ways that are far beyond the reach of any dictionary, and are only beginning to be investigated. When we move beyond single words, the conclusion becomes even more dramatic. Language acquisition seems much like the growth of organs generally; it is something that happens to a child, not that a child does. And while the environment plainly matters, the general course of what happens and the basic features of what emerges are predetermined by the initial state. But the initial state is a common human possession. It must be, then, that in their essential properties and even down to fine detail, languages are cast to the same mold. The Martian scientist might reasonably conclude that there is a single human language, with differences only at the margins.

As languages were more carefully investigated from the point of view of generative grammar, it became clear that their diversity had been underestimated as radically as their complexity and the extent to which they are determined by the initial state of the faculty of language. At the same time, we know that the diversity and complexity can be no more than superficial appearance.

These were surprising conclusions, paradoxical but undeniable. They pose in a stark form what has become the central problem of the modern study of language: How can we show that all languages are variations on a single theme, while at the same time recording faithfully their intricate properties of sound and meaning, superficially diverse? A genuine theory of human language has to satisfy two conditions: 'descriptive adequacy' and 'explanatory adequacy'. The grammar of a particular language satisfies the condition of descriptive adequacy insofar as it gives a full and adequate account of the properties of the language, of what the speaker of the language knows. To satisfy the condition of explanatory adequacy, a theory of language must show how each particular language can be derived from a uniform initial state under the 'boundary conditions' set by experience. In this way, it provides an explanation of the properties of languages at a deeper level.

There is a serious tension between these two research tasks. The search for descriptive adequacy seems to lead to ever greater complexity and variety of rule systems, while the search for explanatory adequacy requires that language structure must be invariant, except at the margins. It is this tension that has largely set the guidelines for research. The natural way to resolve the tension is to challenge the traditional assumption, carried over to early generative grammar, that a language is a complex system of rules, each specific to particular languages and particular grammatical constructions: rules for forming relative clauses in Hindi, verb phrases in Swahili, passives in Japanese, and so on. Considerations of explanatory adequacy indicate that this cannot be correct.

▷ *What do you feel about the following three claims by Chomsky?*

  1 The new words learnt by a small child 'are understood in delicate and intricate ways that are far beyond the reach of any dictionary'.

  2 '... in their essential properties and even down to fine detail, languages are cast to the same mold. The Martian scientist might reasonably conclude that there is a single human language, with differences only at the margins.'

  3 '... the traditional assumption ... that a language is a complex system of rules, each specific to particular languages and particular grammatical constructions: rules for forming relative clauses in Hindi, verb phrases in Swahili, passives in Japanese, and so on ... cannot be correct.'

Text 19

R. L. TRASK: 'Government-and-Binding Theory' in *Key Concepts in Language and Linguistics*. Routledge 1998, pages 108–9

Trask describes the theory, developed in the early 1980s, which incorporated Chomsky's 'Principles and Parameters' model.

Just like transformational grammar, GB [Government-and-Binding Theory] sees every sentence as having both an abstract underlying structure (the former *deep structure*, now renamed *D-structure*), and a superficial structure (the former *surface structure*, now renamed *S-structure*). There is also a third level of representation, called *logical form* (LF). Certain requirements apply to each one of these three levels, while further requirements apply to the way in which the three of them are related.

The motivation for all this, of course, is the hope of reducing the grammars of all languages to nothing more than minor variations upon a single theme, the unvarying principles of universal grammar. But the task is far from easy, and Chomsky, confronted by recalcitrant data, has been forced into the position of claiming that the grammar of every language consists of two quite different parts: a *core*—which alone is subject to the principles of universal grammar—and a *periphery*—consisting of miscellaneous language-specific statements not subject to universal principles. This ploy has been seen by critics as a potentially catastrophic retreat from the whole basis of the Chomskyan research programme.

GB was an abstract framework to begin with, but it has become steadily more abstract, as its proponents, confronted by troublesome data, have tended to posit ever greater layers of abstraction, in the hope of getting their universal principles to apply successfully at some level of representation. Critics have not been slow to see this retreat into abstraction as a retreat from the data altogether, that is as an attempt to shoehorn the data into *a priori* principles which themselves are sacrosanct . The more outspoken critics have declared the GB framework to be more a religious movement than an empirical science. Nevertheless, GB has for years been by far the most influential and widely-practised theory of grammar in existence.

Recently, however, Chomsky has, to general surprise, initiated the *Minimalist Programme*, in which almost all of the elaborate machinery of GB is rejected in favour of a very different approach. It is too early to tell whether GB, like its transformational predecessors, is about to be consigned by its own proponents to the dustbin of history; if this does happen, those critics will surely become even more outspoken in their dismissal of the whole Chomskyan enterprise.

▷ *Is Trask simply setting out Chomsky's views and those of Chomsky's critics, or does he align himself with the critics? If you feel he does this, where in the text do his own views appear?*

▷ *Do you think that human beings have an innate knowledge of universal grammar?*

Text 20

PETER SKEHAN: 'The critical period hypothesis' in *A Cognitive Approach to Language Learning*. Oxford University Press 1998, pages 227–8

Skehan discusses the idea of a 'critical period,' after which normal language learning is impossible, in the light of the case of 'Genie', a child who was deprived of linguistic input by her psychopathic parents until she was rescued at age 13.

Genie was studied intensively during the years after her discovery. She represents a human being exposed to her first language after the age of puberty, and so a terrible test of the Critical Period Hypothesis. For syntax to be still accessible to Genie would mean that the critical period does not exist, and that it is simply being exposed to one's first language that is the crucial issue. For Genie not to acquire syntax would strongly suggest that the part of the brain crucial for language development needs to receive input at a particular phase of the lifespan. So her case is a very important one, which accounts for the special nature of the research project she was at the centre of. She underwent a series of psychological tests and demonstrated a range of cognitive abilities, some of them, such as spatial operations, reaching (at least) the normal level. Genie's language development, however, even after a number of years, and despite adequate input and stimulation, was markedly deviant in many respects. Her acquisition of lexical elements was relatively good, and showed steady and continuous improvement. The development of her ability to produce sentences, in contrast, was severely limited. Her sentences were never more than long strings of simple elements. After eight years of 'normality' she still had not developed effectively in areas of the auxiliary system, of morphology, and of a range of syntactic operations. ... In addition, in Genie's case, language seemed not to be located in specific left hemisphere regions (as is typical in the normal population) but instead seemed to be based in the right hemisphere in a more undifferentiated manner ... . So, many aspects of language, not having experienced the appropriate conditions earlier, did not develop. The timing of the interaction between genetically-programmed development and the necessary input was disturbed and seemed subsequently to become irretrievable.

▷ *Very few adult learners achieve a perfect command of a foreign language. Do you think this is good evidence for the critical period hypothesis, or might it have other causes?*

SECTION 3
References

The references which follow can be classified into introductory level (marked ■□□), more advanced and consequently more technical (marked ■■□), and specialized, very demanding (marked ■■■).

Chapter 1
What is grammar?

■□□
JEAN AITCHISON: *The Seeds of Speech: Language Origin and Evolution*. Cambridge University Press 1996

This book offers an accessible and fascinating examination of possible scenarios for the evolution of language, and explores the nature of the similarities and differences between the world's languages.

■□□
GUY DEUTSCHER: *The Unfolding of Language*. Heinemann 2005

An engagingly written, thoughtful and thought-provoking exploration of language development and change.

■■□
DEREK BICKERTON: *Language and Human Behaviour*. University of Washington Press 1995

Bickerton sees cognition and consciousness as resulting from, rather than preceding, the growth of language via protolanguage.

■■□
ALISON WRAY (ed.): *The Transition to Language*. Oxford
University Press 2002

A good, wide-ranging collection of papers, some rather technical,
exploring the origins of language.

■■□
C. KNIGHT, M. STUDDERT-KENNEDY, and J. HURFORD
(eds.): *The Evolutionary Emergence of Language*. Cambridge
University Press 2000

Another good collection exploring the origins of language.

Chapter 2
From simplicity to complexity: word classes and structures

■□□
DAVID CRYSTAL: *The Cambridge Encyclopedia of Language*.
Cambridge University Press 1997
DAVID CRYSTAL: *The Cambridge Encyclopedia of the
English Language*. Cambridge University Press 2003

Two magisterial reference works: lucid, lavishly illustrated, and
beautifully produced, covering all aspects of language and English
respectively. Indispensable.

■□□
GERALD NELSON: *The Internet Grammar of English*.
University College, London 1998 http://www.ucl.ac.uk/
internet-grammar/

A good, clear introduction to English grammar, with interactive
exercises. Also available on CD-ROM.

■■□
K. BORJARS and K. BURRIDGE: *Introducing English
Grammar*. Arnold 2001

A user-friendly students' introduction to the analysis of the
structure of English.

■■■

K. BROWN and J. MILLER (eds.): *Concise Encyclopedia of Syntactic Theories*. Pergamon 1997

K. BROWN and J. MILLER (eds.): *Concise Encyclopedia of Grammatical Categories*. Pergamon 1999

Two collections of articles from the ten-volume *Encyclopedia of Language and Linguistics* (ed. R. E. Asher, Pergamon 1994). Very valuable reference guides, though many articles are inevitably quite technical.

■■□

R. QUIRK, S. GREENBAUM, G. LEECH, and J. SVARTVIK: *A Comprehensive Grammar of the English Language*. Longman 1985

The classic descriptive grammar of English. Heavyweight (nearly 1,800 pages), but an excellent reference guide.

■■□

R. HUDDLESTON and G. K. PULLUM: *The Cambridge Grammar of the English Language*. Cambridge University Press 2002

Another excellent reference grammar of English. Denser and more complete in some areas than Quirk *et al.* 1985.

Chapter 3
Grammar in the world's languages

■□□

EDWARD SAPIR: *Language: An Introduction to the Study of Speech*. Thomson Learning 1995

One of the earliest and most engaging books on language for the general reader. Originally published in 1921, but still well worth reading.

■□□

JOHN MCWHORTER: *The Power of Babel: A Natural History of Language*. Heinemann 2001

An entertaining and informative look at the ways in which the world's languages organize their affairs.

■□□

GEORGE L. CAMPBELL (ed.): *Compendium of the World's Languages*. Routledge 1991

A good two-volume reference guide: four- to eight-page entries give brief details of the script, phonology, morphology, and syntax of over 300 languages.

■■□

BERNARD COMRIE (ed.): *The Major Languages series*. Routledge 1990

Detailed accounts of the world's major languages. Separate volumes cover the languages of Western Europe; Eastern Europe; East and South-East Asia; and South Asia, the Middle East, and Africa.

■■■

BERNARD COMRIE: *Language Universals and Linguistic Typology: Syntax and Morphology*. Blackwell 1989

An authoritative survey of grammatical features as they are realized in the world's languages. Topics include word order, subject, case marking, relative clauses, causative constructions, and animacy.

Chapter 4
Grammar and vocabulary

■□□

STEVEN PINKER: *Words and Rules*. Perennial 2000

A lucid general survey of language, from an innatist perspective, taking the relationship between vocabulary and grammar as a fundamental reference point.

■■□

ALISON WRAY: *Formulaic Language and the Lexicon*. Cambridge University Press 2002

A clear and very readable study, offering a coherent model of the acquisition, storage, and use of formulaic language.

■■■
NORBERT SCHMITT (ed.): *Formulaic Sequences: Acquisition, Processing and Use.* John Benjamins 2004

A collection of papers on formulaic language, with a psycho-linguistic focus.

Chapter 5
Grammar in spoken and written text

■■□
D. BIBER, S. JOHANSSON, G. LEECH, S. CONRAD, and E. FINEGAN: *Longman Grammar of Spoken and Written English.* Longman 1999

A large, entirely corpus-based grammar of English, with separate analyses of the grammatical characteristics of conversation, fiction, news, and academic prose. Very good treatment of some aspects of spoken language.

■■□
MICHAEL MCCARTHY: *Spoken Language and Applied Linguistics.* Cambridge University Press 1998

A collection of papers dealing principally with the grammar of spoken discourse.

■■■
DAVID BRAZIL: *A Grammar of Speech.* Oxford University Press 1995

An analysis of the grammar of spoken English, showing how discourse is constructed through the interaction of outside-world knowledge with a functionally oriented language system.

Chapter 6
Grammar and language change

■□□
JEAN AITCHISON: *Language Change: Progress or Decay?* (3rd edn.). Cambridge University Press 2001

An authoritative and eminently readable survey of the mechanisms of linguistic change, with examples from a wide range of languages.

■■■

J. BYBEE, R. PERKINS, and W. PAGLIUCA: *The Evolution of Grammar: Tense, Aspect and Modality in the Languages of the World*. University of Chicago Press 1994

A detailed and extremely interesting account of grammaticalization processes at work.

■■■

P. J. HOPPER and E. C. TRAUGOTT: *Grammaticalization*. Cambridge University Press 2003

The second edition of the classic introduction to this subject.

■□□

JOAN C. BEAL: *English in Modern Times*. Arnold 2004

This well-written and informative book on the recent history of English includes a chapter on syntactic change, and one on the history of grammars, grammarians, and attitudes to correctness.

■□□

CHARLES BARBER: *The English Language: A Historical Introduction*. Cambridge University Press 1993

A thorough and accessible one-volume survey of the history of English, ending with a look at English as a world language and a discussion of possible future developments.

■■□

R. HOGG, N. BLAKE, R. LASS, S. ROMAINE, R. BURCHFIELD, and J. ALGEO (eds.): *The Cambridge History of the English Language*. Cambridge University Press 1992–2001

The most complete and definitive survey of the history of English. The six volumes include one on English in North America, and one on world Englishes.

Chapter 7
Grammar in society: 'correctness' and standardization

■□□

STEVEN PINKER: *The Language Instinct*. Allen Lane 1994

A highly readable introduction to linguistics for the general reader, with an innatist bias. Chapter 12, 'The language mavens', is a hard-hitting critique of prescriptivist attitudes.

■□□

JOHN MCWHORTER: *Word on the Street*. Perseus 1998

This engaging and important book is concerned to defend non-standard varieties of American English, including Black English, against prescriptivist attacks.

■□□

E. W. GILMAN (ed.): *Merriam-Webster's Dictionary of English Usage*. Merriam-Webster 1993

Instead of simply attacking the usual targets ('less people', 'between you and I', etc.), the authors, with impressive scholarship, give the history both of the structures in question and of the prescriptive rules that condemn them.

■■□

JAMES MILROY and LESLEY MILROY (eds.): *Real English: The Grammar of English Dialects in the British Isles*. Longman 1993

This book includes chapters on the social and educational issues relating to non-standard English, as well as surveys of the grammar of Scottish, Irish, Southern British, and Tyneside and Northumbrian English.

■□□

TOM MCARTHUR: *The Oxford Guide to World English*. Oxford University Press 2002

A comprehensive guide to worldwide varieties of English, which highlights by implication the parochial nature of British- and American-based prescriptive attitudes.

Chapter 8
Grammar in the head

■□□

JEAN AITCHISON: *The Articulate Mammal: An Introduction to Psycholinguistics*. Routledge 1998

The fourth edition of this classic introduction to psycho-linguistics.

■■□

NOAM CHOMSKY: *On Nature and Language*. Cambridge University Press 2002

This book of essays aimed at the general reader includes 'Perspectives on language and mind', 'Language and the brain', and 'An interview on minimalism'.

■■■

ANDREW RADFORD: *English Syntax: An Introduction*. Cambridge University Press 2004

This is, in fact, an introduction to Chomsky's Minimalist Programme. A good attempt to make generative grammar accessible to the non-specialist, but the discussion is inevitably very technical.

■■■

N. C. ELLIS: 'Frequency effects in language processing' in *Studies in Second Language Acquisition* 2002, Volume 24 (2), pages 143–88

This paper argues for the view that language acquisition is based not on innate knowledge, but on the unconscious frequency-based abstraction of regularities in the input. The same issue of *Studies in Second Language Acquisition* contains other papers responding to Ellis's account.

■■■

MICHAEL TOMASELLO: *Constructing a Language: A Usage-Based Theory of Language Acquisition*. Harvard University Press 2003

A clear and thorough book-length presentation of the theory.

SECTION 4
Glossary

Page references to SECTION 1, Survey, are given at the end of each entry.

accusative *See* **case.**

affix Element added to a word to change its meaning or grammatical function. Affixes include prefixes (e.g. 'un-', 'anti-'), suffixes (e.g. '-ed', '-less'), and infixes (as in German *eingekommen*, 'entered', past participle of *einkommen*). [21]

agent Causative participant in a process, typically encoded as grammatical **subject** in many languages: cf. **patient.**

agglutinating language In agglutinating languages (e.g. Turkish, Navajo, Tamil) words can incorporate complex sequences of morphemes, and the word–**phrase** distinction may not be clear-cut: cf. **inflecting language, isolating language.** [23]

agreement System whereby the form of one word is determined by the form or grammatical class of another. [13] [27]

alienable possession Possession of something not an inherent part or feature of the possessor (e.g. a field or a car); grammatically distinguished in some languages from **inalienable possession.** [29]

analytic language *See* **isolating language.**

anaphoric A pronoun or other **pro-form**, used anaphorically, substitutes for a word or expression used earlier, e.g. 'and I bought *them*', 'I hope *so*'. [42]

animacy Grammatical category involving distinct forms for reference to (some or all) living things, e.g. English 'who'. [29]

aspect Grammatical system for showing how processes and states are viewed, e.g. as completed or ongoing. The distinctions between 'I spoke', 'I was speaking', and 'I have spoken' are aspectual. [26]

auxiliary (verb) Verb with mainly grammatical function, used together with a main verb which carries most of the 'outside world' meaning, e.g. '*is* raining', '*did* not answer', '*has* forgotten'. *See also* **modal auxiliaries.** [11]

bleaching Reduction of meaning resulting from **grammaticalization**, as in the future auxiliary 'will', which no longer means 'want'. [36]

Broca's area Part of the brain near the left ear; damage to Broca's area usually results in ungrammatical speech: cf. **Wernicke's area.** [79]

case Cases (e.g. nominative, accusative, genitive, dative) are forms of nouns and pronouns, and of other words that agree with them, used in **inflecting languages** to indicate grammatical functions (e.g. **subject, object**) or relationships (e.g. possession, goal). [3] [48]

chunk *See* **formulaic language.** [77]

classifier Word used with nouns in some languages to indicate membership of noun class, as in Chinese *liang-ben shu*, 'two-classifier book'. [21]

clause Unit containing a verb form and one or more **noun phrases**, which can communicate information about an action, event, situation, or process: cf. **phrase.** [12]

collocation The 'preferences' that words have for the company of others: for instance we say 'a heavy smoker', 'a bad temper', but not *'a bad smoker', *'a heavy temper'. [35]

competence Capacity for linguistic behaviour: the unconscious knowledge that people have of the rules underlying their languages: cf. **performance.** [72]

conjugation Verb class whose members share a particular set of inflections. [25]

constraint Part of a rule that outlaws ungrammatical over-generalizations. [73]

content word Word (like most nouns, verbs, or adjectives) that refers to something in the outside world: cf. **function word.** [9]

contraction Auxiliary merged with another word, e.g. 'I'll', 'don't'. [65]

core grammar That part of grammar which is claimed to be universal to language and known as part of our genetic endowment: cf. **peripheral grammar**. [77]

corpus (plural: corpora) Searchable electronic database of spoken and/or written texts. [58]

creole Full-scale language which originated as a **pidgin**. [31]

critical period The age range (roughly, up to puberty) after which, it is believed, children's capacity for fully successful language learning 'switches off'. [78]

dative *See* **case**.

declension Class (e.g. of nouns or adjectives) whose members share a particular set of **inflections**. [25]

definiteness A definite item is 'known', identifiable by speaker and hearer, e.g. 'What have you done with *the eggs*?' [26]

derivational morphology Rules for changing words so as to produce a new meaning or word class, e.g. 'happy' → 'unhappy', 'reserve' → 'reservation'. *See* **affix**, **inflection**. [23]

determiner Determiners come before adjectives in noun phrases, and show what part of a general class is being talked about. They include articles ('a', 'the'), possessives ('my', etc.), demonstratives ('this', etc.) and quantifiers (e.g. 'each', 'many', 'all'). [15]

dialect Variety of a language; especially a non-**standard** variety. [28]

direct object Noun phrase whose form or position typically encodes meanings such as 'patient' or 'affected participant', e.g. 'The police have arrested *my brother*': cf. **indirect object**. [25]

discourse Language as put to communicative use in speech or writing. [14]

discourse marker Word or expression used to show the structural or communicative status of a piece of text, e.g. 'finally', 'however', 'by the way'. [46]

elicitation test Way of getting an informant to produce natural examples of language. [73]

ellipsis Leaving out words, e.g. 'Seen Nigel?', 'Yes, I have'. [43]

embedding Using a structure as a component of another structure. [17]

evidentiality Showing the source of a speaker's knowledge grammatically, e.g. by the form of the verb. [29]

feminine *See* **gender**.

finite In languages with tense systems, verb form which carries tense, e.g. 'sees', 'saw': cf. **non-finite**. [17]

first person Form indicating reference to (or including) speaker, e.g. 'I', 'our', 'am': cf. **second person**, **third person**. [23]

formal (grammar) Grammatical theory which takes grammatical forms, rather than functions, as basic: cf. **functional**. [19]

formulaic language Multi-word lexical items ('chunks') which are stored in and retrieved from memory as unanalysed wholes. [37]

function word Word which has a grammatical function rather than outside-world reference, e.g. article or auxiliary verb: cf. **content word**. [7]

functional (grammar) Grammatical theory which takes functions and meanings as basic: cf. **formal (grammar)**. [19]

gender System whereby nouns are divided into grammatically differentiated classes, as in the Russian 'masculine/feminine/neuter' categorization. [3] [22]

generative rule or **grammar** Rule or grammar that can be used to generate (specify) all the grammatical sentences and none of the ungrammatical sentences in the relevant domain. [19] [74]

genitive *See* **case**.

given Term used for information presented as being already known, or as background to what is being communicated: cf. **new**. [44]

grammar Set of devices (word order, inflection, use of function words, intonation contours) needed especially to express certain kinds of necessary meaning that cannot be conveyed by referential vocabulary alone: in particular, relationships between concepts, **participant roles**, and **mood**. These devices are also widely used to encode other relatively abstract meanings such as time relationships, **number**, or **evidentiality**. The term **grammar** is also used for a description or theory of grammar.

grammaticality judgement Way of assessing the grammaticality of a sentence or other linguistic unit by consulting native speakers. [73]

grammaticalization Process whereby a word or expression moves from outside-world reference to a more grammatical function, as in the change from the older use of will ('want') to its modern auxiliary use. [29] [55]

head Word which acts as the core of a phrase and gives it its grammatical character. In the noun phrase 'these big books about phonetics', the noun 'books' is the head. [15]

hierarchical organization Form of organization in which linguistic units are components of higher-level units (e.g. words are components of **phrases**, and phrases are components of **clauses**). [41]

honorific Grammatical or lexical form used to express respect. [3] [47]

inalienable possession Possession of something which is an inherent part or feature of the possessor (e.g. consciousness, size, body part, family relation); grammatically distinguished in some languages from **alienable possession**. [29]

indirect object Noun phrase whose form or position typically encodes a meaning such as 'recipient' or 'goal', e.g. 'I sent *the secretary* all the details': cf. **subject, direct object**. [25]

infix *See* **affix**.

inflecting language Language in which grammatical meanings and relations are largely expressed by **inflections**: cf. **isolating language, agglutinating language**. [23]

inflection Change in the form of a word to signal grammatical relation or meaning, as in English 'word'/'words' or 'buy'/'bought'. [7]

input The language to which learners are exposed, and from which they derive some or all of their linguistic knowledge: cf. **poverty of the stimulus**. [75]

intonation Patterns of voice pitch which add grammatical or other kinds of meaning to structures: cf. **tone**. [7] [46]

intransitive An intransitive verb does not normally have a direct object, e.g. 'sleep', 'wonder'. [26]

isolating language Language such as Mandarin Chinese, in which words do not inflect: cf. **inflecting language, agglutinating language**. [23]

lexical, lexis (To do with) vocabulary. [23] [33]

linguistic relativity The idea that the meaning distinctions expressed in a language reflect and shape its speakers' categorization of reality; often called the 'Sapir-Whorf hypothesis'. [30]

masculine *See* **gender.**

modal To do with **mood.**

modal auxiliaries Group of English auxiliary verbs with particular grammatical characteristics that express meanings mostly relating to certainty or possibility, e.g. 'can', 'may', 'must'. [34]

modifier Word or expression which adds to or limits the meaning of another word or expression, e.g. '*really* sorry', '*green* glass'. [9]

modularity The idea that particular aspects of cognition (e.g. language or grammar) are handled by separate modules in the mind or brain. [78]

mood Grammatical category relating to the informative or communicative status of utterances, e.g. whether they refer to established facts, question, express a supposition or condition, deny, request. [21] [25]

morpheme Smallest meaningful unit of language, e.g. 'un-', '-ed' (bound morphemes), 'out', 'elephant' (free morphemes). [18]

morphology The branch of grammar concerned with the way words change their form to express differences in meaning or grammatical function: cf. **syntax.** [23]

neural network Computer model used to explore the way a group of brain cells might operate. [78]

neuter *See* **gender.**

new Term used for that part of a message which carries the information focus: cf. **given.** [44]

nominalize Make a noun from a verb, e.g. 'erupt' → 'eruption', 'arrive' → 'arrival'. [41]

nominative *See* **case.**

non-finite In languages with **tense** systems, verb form which does not carry tense, e.g. 'waiting', 'broken', 'be': cf. **finite.** [17]

noun phrase (NP) Group of words with a noun as **head.** [11]

number System whereby different forms are used to indicate reference to one and more than one (e.g. 'I'/'we', 'horse'/ 'horses'); some languages have distinct number forms for reference to two (dual), three (trial) or a small number (paucal). [25]

object *See* **direct object, indirect object.**

parameter Hypothesized component of **universal grammar** which provides innate knowledge of the limited possible ways in which a particular aspect of language can operate (e.g. **pro-drop**): cf. **principle**. [75]

part of speech Word class, e.g. noun, preposition, **classifier**. [8]

participant role The role (e.g. **agent, patient**, experiencer, recipient, goal) played by a person or thing in a process. [8]

particle Small function word, e.g. Mandarin Chinese *ma* (interrogative marker). [7]

patient Receptive or affected participant in a process, typically encoded as grammatical **object** in many languages: cf. **agent**. [6]

perfective Verb form expressing completion, e.g. 'I *have written*': cf. **aspect**. [29] [54]

performance Instances of language produced by speakers or writers: cf. **competence**. [72]

peripheral grammar That part of grammar which is not claimed to be universal to language, but belongs to the structure of one or more particular languages: cf. **core grammar**. [77]

person Grammatical system for showing whether reference is, for example, to speaker, hearer(s), or something/somebody else: cf. **first/second/third person**. [25]

phrasal verb Compound verb consisting of a base verb plus a preposition or adverb particle, or both, e.g. 'look at', 'break up', 'get on with'. [48]

phrase Group of words that acts as a constituent in **clause** structure, e.g. **noun phrase, verb phrase**: cf. **clause**. [11]

pidgin Rudimentary contact language used, for example, for trade: cf. **creole**. [52]

poverty of the stimulus The idea that the linguistic input children receive is not enough to explain their knowledge of their mother tongues: cf. **input, learnability**. [75]

prefix *See* **affix**.

principle Hypothesized component of universal grammar which provides innate knowledge of a structural feature common to all languages: cf. **parameter**. [75]

pro-drop In a pro-drop language, pronouns (especially subject pronouns) are not grammatically required. *See also* **parameter**. [76]

pro-form Pronoun or other form used as substitute for a more specific expression, e.g. '*He did*', 'Look at *that*'. [43]

progressive Verb form that presents an action or situation as ongoing, not complete, e.g. 'It *was raining*': cf. **aspect**. [29]

recursion Repeated operation of a grammatical process such as **embedding**. [17]

redundancy Expressing something more completely than is strictly necessary, e.g. marking a **subject** by both position and inflection. [14]

register Level of formality in language. [46] [48]

relative clause Clause modifying a noun phrase, e.g. 'the big man *who is dancing on the table*'. [17]

rule Description or knowledge of a regularity. [3] [33] [66]

Sapir-Whorf hypothesis *See* **linguistic relativity**.

second person Form indicating reference to (or including) hearer, e.g. 'you', 'yourselves', older English 'givest': cf. **first person**, **third person**. [57]

selection criteria Rules specifying what forms can or must be used together with a particular word. For example, the verb 'like' is used with an animate subject and a **direct object**, while the verb 'please' is used with a subject and an animate direct object. [14]

selectional idiom Preferred way of expressing a particular stereotyped or recurrent meaning, e.g. 'I'm being served', 'out of work', 'Can I take a message?'. [37]

semantic To do with meaning. [22]

split infinitive Structure in which an adverb comes between 'to' and an infinitive verb, e.g. 'to boldly go'. [67]

standard (language) Variety favoured for official purposes, generally used in writing, and taught in schools. [54] [64]

structure-dependency The fact that in all languages grammatical processes operate primarily on structures, not single words; seen by some linguists as evidence for innate **universal grammar**. [75]

subject Noun phrase whose form or position typically encodes meanings such as 'agent' or 'causative participant'; also marked by verb agreement in some languages. [13]

substratum Elements in a language which show the influence of an older language once spoken in the same area, e.g. a Welsh accent in English, some structures in Irish English. [54]

suffix *See* **affix**.

syntax The rules governing the ways in which words are assembled into structures: cf. **morphology**. [19]

synthetic language *See* **inflecting language**.

tense Grammatical system for showing time relations through changes in the forms of verbs. [25]

third person Form indicating reference to somebody/something other than speaker or hearer, e.g. 'they', 'goes': cf. **first person, second person**. [23]

tone The use of differences of voice pitch on individual words to signal differences of meaning or grammatical function: cf. **intonation**. [48]

topic What an utterance is 'about'. Topic has separate grammatical status in some languages; in English it is most often encoded as **subject**. [35]

transitive A transitive verb normally has a direct object, e.g. 'cut', 'improve': cf. **intransitive**. [14]

universal grammar (UG) Hypothesized innate knowledge of the universal structural features underlying the grammar of all languages. [75]

usage Term used especially in the discussion of variable aspects of language (e.g. formal versus informal), or elements about which there is disagreement. [38] [65]

usage-based associative learning The idea that language acquisition proceeds only from exposure to, and unconscious analysis of, linguistic input. [77]

verb phrase (VP) (In this book): group of words consisting of one or more auxiliary verbs together with a main verb (e.g. 'is waiting', 'would have realized'), or a one-word main verb (e.g. 'spoke'). Used by some grammarians for a verbal group together with its objects and/or complements (e.g. 'is taking photos of all the people from head office'). [11]

vernacular Casual, informal, or non-standard variety of language. [48]

voice The category that includes active and passive. [25]

Wernicke's area Part of the brain near the left ear. Damage to Wernicke's area results in speech which is seriously disrupted in terms of content, but remains fluent and grammatical: cf. **Broca's area**. [79]

'wh'-extraction The grammatical process, or type of structure, in which a 'wh'-word appears outside the clause in which it has a grammatical function, e.g. 'Who do you think Mary was hoping *that John would invite*'. [73]

Acknowledgements

The author and publisher are grateful to those who have given kind permission to reproduce the following excerpts and adaptations of copyright material:

Blackwell Publishing Ltd. for the excerpt from pages 134–5 'On the Inseparability of Grammar and the Lexicon: Evidence from Acquisition' by Elizabeth Bates and Judith C. Goodman from *Language Development*, Blackwell 2001.

Cambridge University Press for the excerpt from 'Gradience' by David Crystal in *The Cambridge Encyclopedia of Language* 2nd edition, CUP 1997.

Cambridge University Press and Dr. Alison Wray for the excerpt from 'How far can you go? Modelling the relationship between grammar and lexis' based on ideas from *Formulaic language and the lexicon* by Alison Wray, CUP 2002.

Cambridge University Press and the author for the excerpt from 'Units of description in grammar and discourse' from *Spoken Language and Applied Linguistics* by Michael McCarthy, © CUP 1998.

Cambridge University Press and the author for the excerpts from *Language Change: Progress or Decay?*, 3rd edition 2001 by Jean Aitchinson, © CUP 2001.

Cambridge University Press for the excerpts from *New Horizons in the Study of Language and Mind* by Noam Chomsky, CUP 2000, © Aviva Chomsky and Eric F. Menoya as Trustees of the Diane Chomsky Irrevocable Trust.

David Higham Associates for the excerpt from 'Poem in October' by Dylan Thomas from *Collected Poems* 1934–52, Dent 1952.

Elsevier for the excerpt reprinted from pages xiv–xv *Concise Encyclopedia of Syntactic Theories* by K. Brown and J. Miller (eds), Pergamon 1996.

Harcourt, Inc for the excerpt from *Language: An Introduction to the Study of Speech* by Edward Sapir, copyright 1921 by Harcourt, Inc. and renewed 1949 by Jean V. Sapir.

John Benjamins Publishing Company, Amsterdam/Philadelphia for the excerpt from page 27 in 'Facilitating the acquisition of formulaic sequences' in N. Schmitt (ed) *Formulaic Sequences*, John Benjamins Publishing Company 2004. www.benjamins.com.

MIT Press for the excerpt from page 4, 'Whither Whorf' in *Language in Mind* by Dedre Gentner and S. Goldin-Meadow, MIT Press 2003.

Oxford University Press for the excerpt from 'Description versus prescription' from *Applied Linguistics* by G. Cook, © OUP 2003.

Oxford University Press for the excerpt from 'The critical period hypothesis' in *A Cognitive Approach to Language Learning* by Peter Skehan, © OUP 1998.

Pearson Education for the excerpt from *English Corpus Linguistics* by K. Aijmer and B. Altenberg (eds), Pearson Education Limited © 1991.

Penguin Group (UK) for the excerpt from *The Language Instinct: The New Science of Language and Mind* by Steven Pinker, Allen Lane/Penguin Press 1994. Copyright © Steven Pinker, 1994.

Random House Group Ltd. for the excerpt from *The Power of Babel* by John McWhorter, Heinemann 2001.

Taylor & Francis Group for the excerpt from Chapter 16 *Introduction to Mathematical Philosophy* by Bertrand Russell, Allen and Unwin 1919.

Taylor & Francis Group for the excerpt from page 540 *History of Western Philosophy* by Bertrand Russell (first published 1946), Routledge 2004.

Taylor & Francis Group for the excerpt from pages 108–9 *Key Concepts in Language and Linguistics* by R. L. Trask, Routledge 1998.

University of Chicago Press for the excerpt from *Language and Species* by Derek Bickerton ©, University of Chicago Press 1990.

Source
Extract from *Old Man and the Sea* by Ernest Hemingway, Arrow 1994.